Paper Plus

UNIQUE PROJECTS

USING

HANDMADE PAPER

NANCY WORRELL

krause publications

700 East State Street • Iola, WI 54990-0001

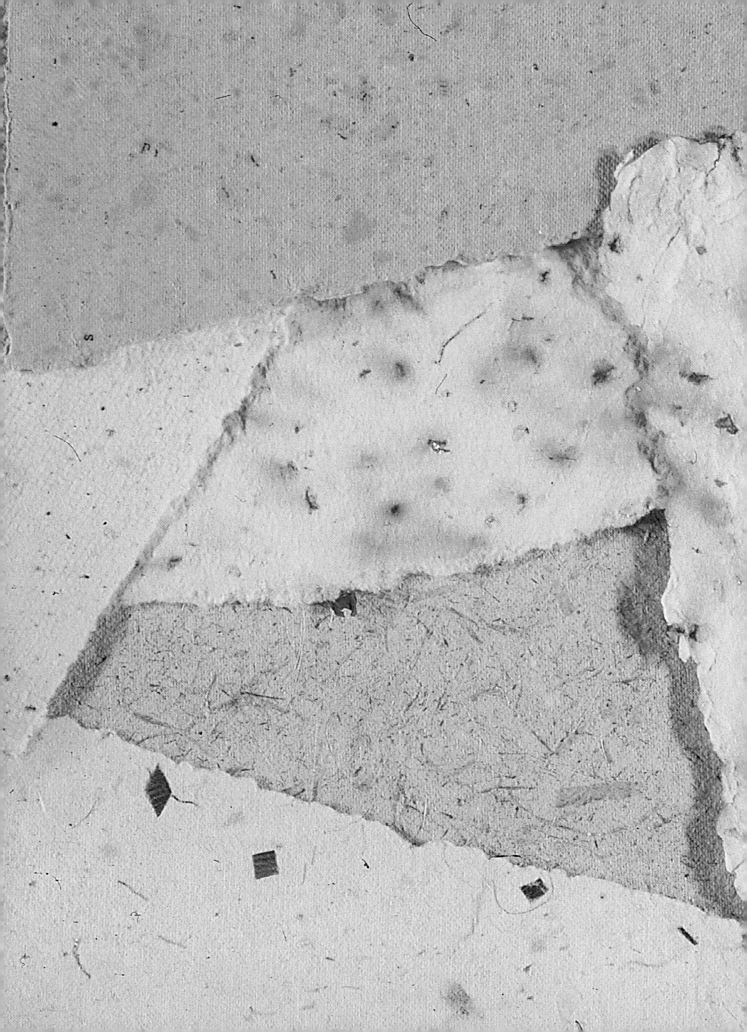

**krause
publications**

700 East State Street • Iola, WI 54990-0001
Telephone 715-445-2214

Please call or write for our free catalog of publications. Our toll-free number to place an order or obtain a free catalog is 800-258-0929 or please use our regular business telephone 715-445-2214 for editorial comment and further information.

Designed by Jan Wojtech
Cover Design by Kim Schierl
Photography by Lynn Ruck
Illustrations by Barbara A.C. Hennig
Manufactured in the United States of America

Library of Congress Cataloging-in-Publication Data

Worrell, Nancy
        Paper plus: unique projects using handmade paper / Nancy Worrell.
        p.   cm.
        Includes bibliographical references and index.
        ISBN 0-8019-8918-3
        1. Papermaking   2. Handmade Paper   3. Title

                                                97-073032
                                                CIP

Acknowledgments

A special thank you to my daughter Heidi, who told me I could; to my husband Frank, who encourages me on a daily basis; and to my friend Vicki, who introduced me to the craft of papermaking. I also want to acknowledge the Society of Craft Designers and their members for their ongoing support.

I also wish to acknowledge the great work and support of my photographer, Lynn Ruck, my illustrator, Barbara Henning, and last but not least Barbara Case, my editor. Thanks for your help in putting together a great book.

And thanks to the following companies, who have been so generous in providing product for use in many of the projects in this book:

Beacon Chemical Co.
Cotton Press
Delta Technical Coatings, Inc.
The DMC Corp.
Duncan Enterprises
Greg Markim, Inc.
Hunt Manufacturing Co.
Kreinik Manufacturing Co., Inc.
Kiti
Paper Chase
Plaid Enterprises, Inc.
Therm O Web

Table of Contents

Part One: Getting Ready

Part Two: Techniques

Part Three:
Projects

Introduction

If you're like me, you've looked at richly textured sheets of paper, and delicate hand-cast paper figures and thought, "I wish I could do that, but…" Well, you can! Making beautiful paper is quite easy and requires a minimum of inexpensive equipment and a little time.

To begin with, you must like having your hands in water—lots of water. My first encounter with papermaking was on a hot July afternoon. The paper pieces were soaked, torn, and pulped. I only had to learn to dip the deckle and mold into the pulp to make my own handmade paper. After many hits and misses, I finished the afternoon, tired and wet, but with some lovely sheets of my very own paper. I was hooked!

I think I've always been fascinated with handmade papers. Like fabrics, papers each have a unique texture and color and are a pleasure to see and touch. I have read books, even worked for a commercial paper company, but the idea

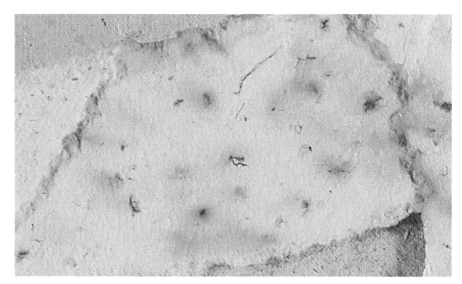

of making my own paper seemed out of reach—it all looked so difficult.

That July afternoon was an eye-opener. Papermaking doesn't require large expensive equipment, nor is it an exact science. Now, armed with my experience, I went back to the library to learn more and expand my experimentation. Much to my dismay, most of the books on papermaking still made the process sound frighteningly complicated. The books described a long arduous endeavor, with most of the recipes calling for plant fibers that can require weeks, even months, to process. And the final products were elaborate bound books of paper or large complex pieces of art.

Not to be discouraged, I continued to make paper that summer and the following summer. During the winter months, I looked for more material on papermaking, finding a chapter here and there in paper

craft books. Most of these books only touched on papermaking and the projects were almost exclusively cards and gift tags. As I looked more closely at the paper craft books, I realized that I could adapt handmade paper to most of the paper craft projects.

I began to experiment—making ornaments and garlands, adding fabrics and laces and treating paper much as I would fabric. I stitched a collage of papers to cover a notebook and a trinket box. Through the craft industry I was introduced to hand-cast papers that added yet another dimension to the sheets of paper I'd been working with. And then I saw sculptures of chicken wire covered in paper pulp. Wow, what an idea!

Clients began showing more interest in my papermaking projects than in my needlework. In fact, I find that all my recent work is papermaking projects. Easy papermaking books for the average crafter are limited. I am an average crafter. I like learning new skills, but I don't have a lot of time nor do I want to spend a lot of money on a new craft until I know it's something I really like to do.

My hope is that this book addresses the needs of the average crafter—an informative, easy manual for discovering the art and craft of papermaking. Please use this book as an inspirational guide, to experience the joy of making your own beautiful papers, and then incorporate those papers into easy and useful objects of art.

Happy Papermaking!

Nancy Worrell

How Paper is Made

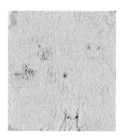

The majority of the paper we use is machine-made from the pulp of soft fibrous woods such as spruce and pine. Cotton and linen are used to make a finer, heavier quality paper, generally used for stationery. Many natural materials such as grasses, hemp, and jute are used to make wrapping papers and other coarse papers. Chemically treated wood fiber is the basis for newsprint.

Today, making handmade paper is considered an art form and the exciting and beautiful uses for handmade paper reflect true artistry. Today's papermakers choose from a large selection of natural fibers and recycled goods to produce handmade paper. They look to the qualities of the paper itself—color, texture, and fiber—and choose their materials accordingly.

The basic process of papermaking hasn't changed much from the first pulping efforts in China some 2,000 years ago. For the projects in this book, you will follow the same steps that have been used for hundreds of years, breaking down the fibers of the base material—be it used computer paper or iris leaves—by soaking or cooking, then blending them with water to produce a smooth creamy pulp. To make sheets from the pulp, you'll either pour it or screen it. To make a hand-cast piece, you'll fill a mold with pulp, and to create dipped sculpture, you'll dip a form, such as a wire basket, into a vat of pulp. All of these techniques have been around for centuries and you can do them all in your home, usually with the tools and equipment already there.

Fun Facts

❖ We are surrounded by paper. Over 350 million magazines, two billion books, and 24 billion newspapers are printed on paper each year. Paper is used for money, checks, and official documents. Almost everything is packaged and shipped in paper containers. Paper is a key ingredient in building materials such as insulation, gypsum board, wallpaper, flooring, and shingles. There is even paper in our television sets and in the remote control batteries.

❖ Ancient cultures used everything from stone, metal and wood, to cloth and tree leaves to record written information. As early as 4000 BC, the Sumerians used clay as a writing surface. Many cultures, including those found in the Himalayas, Americas, and the Pacific Rim, used tree bark, and the peoples of India and Southeast Asia used tree leaves to record Buddhist scriptures and law. In India and Southeast Asia, palm leaves and birch barks were pounded into a writing surface.

❖ The word paper is derived from the Greek and Latin words for papyrus, a plant that grows along the Nile. Papyrus most closely resembles paper as we know it today. By 2800 BC the Egyptians were using papyrus for making a writing surface. The fibrous papyrus stems were peeled and the pith sliced and pounded into strips. These strips were laid cross-wise, dampened, beaten, and pressed into sheets of paper which were polished with stone, bone, or shell for a smooth surface. Papyrus remained the primary writing surface until medieval Europe.

❖ The first paper pulping process occurred in China in AD 105. The Chinese used the bark of mulberry trees, hemp waste, fishing nets, and ropes to make paper. They washed, soaked, and beat the material, then poured a thin layer onto a woven cloth stretched across a bamboo frame to dry. Chinese papermakers are also credited with first using starch as sizing on the paper to prevent ink from bleeding into the paper grains.

TIMELINE

2800 BC	105 AD	610	1150
Egyptians began using papyrus for writing	Pulped paper invented by Chinese	Papermaking introduced to Japan	Papermaking introduced to Spain

1221	1456	1690	1714
Holy Roman Emperor Frederick II declared all official documents written on paper invalid	Printing of Gutenberg Bible	First paper mill in America at Germantown, Pennsylvania	Invention of typewriter

1798	1809	1842	1874
First practical papermaking machine	First cylinder paper machine devised by John Dickinson in England	First Christmas card in England	First United States greeting card produced

CIRCA 1900	1928	1951	1974
All paper produced in America was machine-produced	Mill for producing handmade paper established by Dard Hunter	Computers first applied to business uses	Word processing begins to replace typewriter

Part One:

Getting Ready

Equipment

ost of the equipment for papermaking is already in your home. You'll need a bucket, a colander/strainer, a blender or food processor, a rolling pin, and absorbent fabric pieces called felts. You'll also need plastic storage vats to use as pulp vats and a deckle and mold—which is simply two wooden frames, one with screening stretched over it.

For hand-cast projects, you'll need molds. Chances are, you already have a variety of molds in your kitchen—cookie cutters, gelatin molds, and decorative muffin tins are good examples.

Sculpture projects require an armature—a skeleton or framework. Typical examples include wire baskets or wire figures, which you can purchase or create yourself.

Before purchasing equipment, do a thorough search through your cupboards and storage areas. You'll be surprised at how much usable equipment you've put into storage and forgotten. If you do need to purchase some things, check out yard sales and consignment shops before buying new items.

Here are some specifics on the equipment you'll need.

You'll need a *bucket* to soak your papermaking materials, to hold drain water from the pulp, to dip armatures, and during clean up. The bucket should be large enough to accommodate large pieces of paper and deep enough to use for dipping a wire basket or other armature. Because you can't soak different colors of paper together, you'll want a separate bucket for each color.

A *colander* or *wire mesh strainer* is essential for draining water from wet pulp.

You'll use a *blender or food processor* to pulverize the soaked materials into pulp. A heavy-duty kitchen blender works fine—if you are careful not to overload it. It's best to have a blender that you use just for papermaking. I picked up a used blender at a garage sale for a few dollars.

You'll need *bins* or *vats* to hold and store the pulp. I suggest you buy at least one 28-quart vat, (the usual size of an under-bed storage container) and a few smaller ones (sweater box size). Buy vats with lids to keep the pulp clean and to cover it between work sessions.

To eliminate the water from the pulp and to mesh the fibers together into a smooth sheet of paper, you'll need to roll or press the wet paper pulp with a *rolling pin* or a long round bottle, such as a wine bottle. Some papermaking kits include a plastic screen and a pressing bar for this purpose.

A *flower press* or similar device will also come in handy for pressing water from handmade paper. A press can be as simple as two wooden boards with bricks stacked on top, so you don't need to buy a special device if you don't already have one.

Among the most important pieces of equipment for papermaking are the *felts*—absorbent pieces of either wool or synthetic felt or other fabrics. Some papermaking kits include heavy blotter sheets, but you can easily use old towels or wool blankets. The best felts are absorbent and strong enough to hold the paper when you carry it to the drying area. Wool felt is the most absorbent, but synthetic felt, some cotton fabrics, and old towels work well too.

Be sure to consider the texture of the felts, because it will be impressed into the paper when you roll or press paper between them. This can be wonderful or horrible, depending on the effect you want and the texture of the felt.

> **HOT TIP**
> *Make your own felts from an old woolen blanket by cutting the blanket into pieces just larger than the size of paper sheets you will be making—12" x 14" is a good size. Use your sewing machine to zigzag stitch around the edges to prevent fraying.*

A *deckle* and *mold* are essential for making sheets of paper. The deckle is an open frame that defines the edges of the paper sheet, and the mold is a screen-covered frame used to collect the pulp for forming the paper sheet. The size of the sheet of paper will be determined by the inner dimension of the deckle frame.

You can make a deckle and mold unit easily with canvas stretcher bars, available at most art and craft supply stores. (See "Constructing a Deckle and Mold" on page 14.)

An easy and inexpensive alternative is to stretch a fiberglass screen or nylon net over a plastic or wooden embroidery hoop. Trim the overlap of screen or net around the edge of the embroidery hoop because the pulp will cling to it. Though embroidery hoops are generally limited to round or oval shapes, you may be able to find rectangular hoops, which are sometimes used to frame finished needlework projects.

An embroidery hoop with screen.

Plastic lids from coffee cans or plastic containers make quick, inexpensive screens. Trim away the inner circle of plastic so that only the outer rim remains. Stretch a fiberglass screen or nylon net over the opening and snap the lid on the can. This type of screen works great for pouring sheets, where you pour a small amount of pulp on the screen to spread out in a thin sheet. Because of its size and lack of a frame, it won't work for screening sheets of paper, where you drag the screen through a vat of pulp and water to collect a thin layer of pulp on the screen.

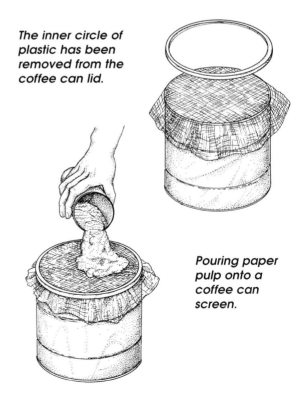

The inner circle of plastic has been removed from the coffee can lid.

Pouring paper pulp onto a coffee can screen.

For hand-cast projects, you'll need a few *molds*. Molds are available in many different materials, sizes, and shapes and it's likely you have some in your kitchen that will work fine with paper pulp. Be creative. Look in your kitchen or the children's toy box for molds. For papermaking, the top of the mold must be larger than the bottom so that you can get the dried paper pulp out of it without destroying the piece.

Beginners may want to start with plastic molds, which are generally less detailed and relatively inexpensive. Some papermaking kits include simple plastic molds. Other mold alternatives include candy and gelatin molds and decorative muffin tins. Clear plastic molds are nice because you can see if the pulp has filled in all the details. Another advantage of plastic molds is flexibility—a little bending and the hand-cast paper will pop out of the mold. The one disadvantage is that it takes the pulp a long time to dry in plastic and you can't speed it up by heating it in the oven.

Terra cotta molds are available from a number of suppliers and come in a variety of designs, from very simple shapes to very detailed designs. Hand-cast paper projects from these molds resemble plaster molds and are usually beautifully detailed.

While cookie cutters are not considered molds, you can use them as such. I generally use the metal type of cookie cutter that's open on both the top and bottom. This type serves as a "frame" for the pulp. If you can't find a cookie cutter in the shape you want, cut your own design into a piece of foam board. Look in coloring books for simple shapes to copy.

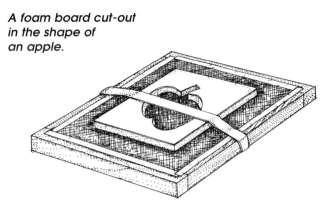

A foam board cut-out in the shape of an apple.

You probably have some plastic cookie cutters that press a design into the dough and cut out the shape at the same time. You can use these for hand-casting too. Remember to spray them with nonstick cooking spray and to fill them enough to overflow the mold so that you'll have enough of an edge to help you get it out of the mold.

To create dipped sculpture, you'll need some sort of *armature*. You can create a free-form sculpture by bending and twisting chicken wire or other fine mesh wire into a unique and interesting shape. Gift shops and garden centers carry wire baskets and other forms you can use as armatures, but be sure the wire has been treated to protect against rust because paper pulp is largely water and any rust that occurs will seep through the paper pulp on your beautiful sculpture.

Save plastic berry baskets from the grocery store or use loosely woven baskets, shown right, open weave cane baskets, or vine wreaths. Tie twigs together and dip. Use your imagination—the possibilities are infinite.

Preparing Papermaking Equipment

As we've already established, you'll need a few common pieces of equipment and a few specialty items for papermaking. You probably already have a bucket, a colander/strainer, and a rolling pin. You'll also need a heavy-duty blender or food processor, vats, and felts to hold the newly made paper sheets while drying. For hand-cast or dipped projects, have the molds or ready-to-use armatures close at hand before beginning the papermaking process.

It's important that the bucket you use for papermaking be clean and large enough to hold the water you'll drain off the pulp. If you plan to dip sculpt, the bucket should be large enough to hold the armature without crowding. Remember, you can't pour waste water down the drain, so you'll need a bucket with a sturdy handle to haul the waste water away.

The colander/strainer should also be clean and free from any oils or other food stuffs.

A heavy-duty kitchen blender or food processor is ideal for making paper. If you plan to make a lot of paper, I recommend you purchase a blender or food processor to use only for papermaking. Thoroughly clean the blender before and after each use because any debris left in the blender will become part of the next batch of paper you pulp. Because the blender will be coming in contact with both electricity and water, take all necessary precautions associated with using an electrical appliance near water. Be sure to keep all electrical connections dry.

Assemble the vats you need and make sure they are clean and water tight.

Buy or construct a deckle and mold. (Instructions for constructing a deckle and mold are on page 14.) Again, the deckle and mold should be thoroughly cleaned of any debris left from previous papermaking sessions.

Make or purchase a sufficient number of felts in varying sizes. Wool felts are the most absorbent, but synthetic felts, absorbent cottons and old towels also work well, as does heavy blotter paper.

Wool felts can be expensive, so check your sewing cabinet for leftovers from sewing projects, or buy a large woolen blanket at a garage sale. Make sure the material you plan to use is clean and dry. Cut it into squares just larger than the sheets of paper you want to make—cut a 10" x 12" felt for an 8" x 11" sheet of paper. To prevent fraying, zigzag stitch around the edges of the squares. Prepare at least two to four felts for every sheet of paper and even more if you plan to stack them with paper sheets in a press to dry.

If you're doing hand-casting, thoroughly wash and dry the molds and spray them with nonstick cooking spray or a spray especially formulated for papermaking. Wipe away any excess with a soft cloth or paper towel, making sure that all the nooks and crannies have been coated.

You can easily use clean metal or plastic cookie cutters to shape the paper pulp if they are open on both the top and bottom. Just rubber band the cookie cutter on the mold to hold it in place and to prevent the pulp from seeping under the edges. Spray the inside of the cookie cutter with nonstick cooking spray before filling it with pulp.

If you plan to cut out your own designs from foam board, do so before beginning the papermaking process. It's not necessary to treat foam board with nonstick spray before adding the paper pulp because the foam board will be removed before the pulp dries.

For dip sculpting, have the wire armatures ready to go before beginning the papermaking process.

> ## HOT TIP
> *When working indoors, do the couching in a cookie pan or other large shallow baking pan lined with newspapers or old towels to absorb the water.*

Making a Deckle & Mold

To screen handmade paper sheets, construct the deckle and mold as shown on the next page. The dimensions of the deckle will determine the size of your finished sheet of paper, so buy stretcher bars 1½" longer than the size paper you want to make. For example, to screen an 8" x 11" sheet of paper, use 12" and 14" stretcher bars. If you plan to make cards or stationery, it's best to make standard size paper (5" x 7" or 8" x 11") so it will fit in a purchased envelope. Of course, you can cut or tear larger sheets to any size.

The deckle and mold made with stretcher bars will work great for screening, but you'll need a deeper deckle for pouring. When pouring instead of screening, you'll float the deckle in a vat of water and pour paper pulp into it, so you'll need a deckle deep enough to hold an inch of water above the screen to float the pulp on. You can make a pouring deckle with 2"-wide boards rather than stretcher bars, the same dimensions as the mold, or you can purchase a deckle and mold made specifically for the pouring method.

YOU WILL NEED:

- 8 canvas stretcher bars (1½" longer than the paper sheets you want to make)
- Waterproof wood glue
- Sealer
- Paint brush to apply sealer
- Fiberglass screen to fit mold size
- Staples or tacks
- Staple gun or hammer
- Duct tape (optional)
- Weather stripping tape (optional)

1. To form the frame for the deckle, apply glue along the tongue and groove fitting on four of the stretcher bars and fit them together. Let the glue dry completely.

Fit the stretcher bars together to form a frame.

2. To form the frame for the mold, apply glue along the tongue and groove fitting on four of the stretcher bars and fit them together. Let the glue dry completely.

3. Paint several coats of sealer on the deckle and mold frames, allowing each coat to dry completely before applying the next.

4. Tightly stretch a piece of screen over one frame to make the mold. Begin at one corner, working around the frame in both directions. Holding tight, tack or staple the screen to the frame. Trim off any excess screen hanging over the edge of the mold.

After the fiberglass screen has been stretched over the mold frame, staple it in place and trim the excess.

5. Although it isn't necessary, it's a good idea to cover the staples and sharp edges with duct tape.

Cover the staples with duct tape.

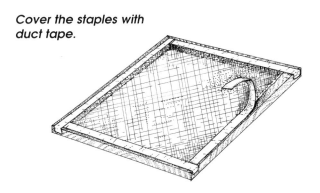

6. Optional: Cut a length of weather stripping to fit the inside of the deckle edge and glue it in place. This will make a tighter seal between the deckle and mold when screening. Using a mold with weather stripping applied will result in a sheet of paper with smoother edges.

Attach weather stripping to the inside of the deckle.

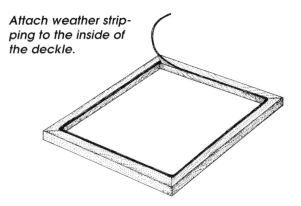

Preparing Your Work Space

When setting up your work space, keep in mind that papermaking is very wet and messy, so you'll need someplace waterproof and easy to mop. It's most convenient to use a place where you don't have to clean up and put everything away after each work session.

You'll need a convenient water source, an electrical outlet, and a table or flat working surface. Keep in mind that you can't pour waste water down the drain, so you'll need to haul it outdoors. (I pour my waste water in flower beds or along the edge of the yard. Linter is a natural cotton fiber and won't hurt the environment but it will show, so try to find a spot where it won't be unsightly.)

You should have enough space for the bucket, the blender or food processor, the large vat of pulp and the felts, which will hold the wet paper. And remember that as you carry the felts to the drying area they will drip, so try to avoid a path through your living room or other carpeted areas. The closer to the drying area, the better.

In nice weather, there's no better place for papermaking than your deck, screened-in porch, or garage. Of course, you can use the kitchen or bathroom, but the clean up might be a bit overwhelming because you will inevitably spatter, spill, and splash.

Choosing a Drying Area

When the time comes for drying, remember that the felt pieces and paper pulp are going to be very wet. The drying area must tolerate moisture, preferably have low humidity, and be free of dust and debris.

For outdoor drying, you'll need a flat

surface off the ground and extra felt pieces to cover the paper to protect it from falling debris. Avoid drying paper in direct sunlight because the sun will cause fading and curling, especially if the handmade paper is colored with construction paper.

Using a press to dry paper requires less room but a longer drying period. In a press, you stack paper sheets between dry felts, tighten the clamps and wait. Drying can take as long as a week, depending on climate conditions. High heat and low humidity may speed up the process.

Storing Pulp and Finished Paper

To save time and clean up, you may want to make large batches of pulp in one session to use over several days or months. Most paper pulp will keep for a couple of days if stored at room temperature in a covered vat, but not much longer. Pulp from plants, pulp with recycled papers, or pulp with added plant fibers will very likely ferment if left for several days at room temperature.

If you aren't planning to work with the pulp within a week, drain off as much water as possible and store it in containers in the refrigerator or freezer. It's best to use refrigerated pulp within a month and frozen pulp within a year.

For long term storage, you should either freeze or dry the pulp. To dry it, first strain it through a colander, drain it in a hanging cheesecloth and leave it hanging until dry. This dried lump of pulp can be stored indefinitely and will break apart easily when you're ready to use it.

Storing finished handmade paper is a bit tricky because it's very fragile. If you have an extra file cabinet, you can store sheets in file folders labeled by color and/or paper content. Empty number 10 envelope boxes or 8" x 11" stationery boxes are excellent for storing handmade paper sheets. You can store hand-cast paper loosely in a box in a dry area.

Materials

HOT TIP

Keep your eyes open for surfaces you can use for embossing a design into the paper. Woven mats, embossed felts, lace, net, and screens all add texture to the surface of the paper. Laying wet sheets of paper on the fronds of a fern will make a lovely impression of the fern. Experiment with other surfaces to see how they effect the texture of your paper.

Part of the fun of papermaking is using different materials in the pulp. Depending on your preference, you might choose natural materials, recycled materials, household fibers, or purchased materials. Combining materials adds strength, texture, and color.

The most common fiber used in papermaking is cotton linter, available from craft or art supply stores. Inexpensive and easy to use, cotton linter is 100% cotton fibers that are too short to use for thread-spinning. You can use pulp made entirely of cotton linter, or use the cotton linter pulp as a base, adding various ingredients to create different effects. The advantage of using at least some cotton linter in the pulp is that it adds strength and is easy to mix. Most papermaking kits include sheets of cotton linter or you can buy small packages of it at craft or art supply stores.

Of course you can make pulp entirely out of recycled materials too. Office papers, white computer paper, and colored flyers can all be pulped to make handmade paper. Gift wrap, colored tissue paper, and construction paper will add color and texture to handmade paper. Start saving paper—bits of paper doilies, business cards, matte finish greeting cards, etc. Just about any paper product (with the exception of glossy paper) can be pulped to make handmade paper.

Natural material such as dried grass and leaves, onion and garlic skins, and prepared natural fibers such as celery, rhubarb, asparagus, and okra can be processed and added to the pulp for texture and color. Dried flower petals and tiny seeds, such as lavender, can be added to the pulp and screened or laminated onto the sheet of wet paper.

Don't forget to save snippets of sewing thread, embroidery floss, and metallic fibers to add to the pulp. Tiny bits of fabric, ribbon, lace, and even dryer lint will add interest to your handmade papers.

HOT TIP

Keep a box next to your sewing and craft work areas for collecting threads from stitching, bits of fabric trimmings, snippets of ribbon, bits of paper, glitter and potpourri from other projects. When you're ready to make paper, you will already have collected a wonderful array of things to add.

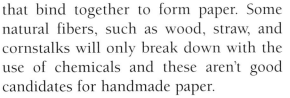

Materials from Nature

There are three types of natural fibers that can be used in papermaking—bast, leaf, and grass. All of them must be cooked to soften and break down the fibers and to release the cellulose fibers that bind together to form paper. Some natural fibers, such as wood, straw, and cornstalks will only break down with the use of chemicals and these aren't good candidates for handmade paper.

Bast fibers come from the inner bark of the plant and are long, slender, and strong. Examples of bast fibers are okra, kudzu, elm, lilac, and mulberry. To harvest the fibers from these plants you must first strip them and then wait for them to decompose to recover the usable fibrous material or use soda lye or caustic soda to break them down. Although these fibers produce strong translucent sheets of paper, they aren't practical for the home papermaker.

Leaf fibers are shorter, more opaque, and generally produce paper with a rough texture. Leaf fibers often need to be scraped to remove their tough outer layer before cooking. Examples of leaf fibers are sisal, pineapple, and yucca leaves.

Grass fibers are short and brittle and the yield from dry grass fibers is low. Because many have hollow stems, these fibers are more difficult to cook. Cornstalks and bamboo are examples of grass fibers to try.

After mastering the basic technique of papermaking using recycled papers and/or cotton linter, you may want to experiment with local plant fibers. Most

papermakers who use plant fibers for papermaking also use soda lye or caustic soda to break down the plant fibers. These chemicals cause burns if they come in contact with your skin and must be cooked in stainless steel or cast iron pots. The cooked materials must be thoroughly rinsed to remove the chemicals.

I prefer not to use hazardous materials in my paper, so I make paper that incorporates cooked plant fibers without using chemicals. Instead, I dice and chop the plants, then cook the materials until mushy and blend them into a fine pulp. Because it requires so much plant fiber to make paper, I add cotton linter, making a mixture of 1/1 cooked plant fibers and cotton linter. An example of this is the Iris Leaf paper (recipe on page 48).

Take a tour of your yard, garden, and supermarket. Look for fibrous vegetables and leaves such as onions, leeks, celery, okra, rhubarb, and iris leaves. Try boiling and blending autumn leaves, grass clippings, and corn husks. Experiment with various plants indigenous to your area and keep a diary to record the results. Check your local library for books on plant fibers and papermaking.

Materials from the Recycling Bin

Making handmade paper from used paper is a great way to recycle. Using different types and colors will produce interesting textures and colors in your handmade paper. If you don't thoroughly pulverize printed paper, the print will often appear in the finished product, giving it some added interest. Gift wrap

and tissue papers add color and sometimes surprising texture.

High quality stationery and card stock with a high rag content will produce strong, long lasting paper. Less expensive papers, such as typing and computer paper, are suitable, but it's a good idea to add cotton linter to the paper pulp for added strength and durability.

Don't use glossy magazine pages or color brochures, as they will become gray and gummy during the pulping process. You can add tiny pieces of magazine pages to the pulp just before screening, but not during pulping.

Newspaper and most recycled papers have a high acid content and will become brittle and deteriorate quickly, so avoid using these for projects that you want to last for a long time. As with all things, high quality materials yield high quality results.

Preparing Papermaking Materials

Whatever materials you use to make paper must be prepared before you can begin to pulp. This generally means tearing and soaking paper for a period of time. Grocery bags, produce cartons, and cotton linter must be torn or cut into strips and soaked overnight.

If the paper is hard to tear or if you have a large quantity to tear, soak it for two to three hours before tearing it into one-inch pieces for pulping. Presoaked paper is much easier to tear. When making a small quantity of pulp from computer paper, stationery, or other office papers, tear the paper into one-inch pieces as you go.

Natural materials such as grass, leaves, and skins will add interesting texture and color to your handmade paper and are fun to include. You'll need to cook most natural materials before pulping to soften and break them down. The amount of cooking time varies with the thickness of the plant, but they should be cooked until they're soft and mushy and can be easily pulped.

Some fibers, such as onion and garlic skins, don't require cooking if they're finely chopped and added to pulp just before screening.

Flower petals and seeds work best when added to the pulp vat and screened rather than pulped with the paper. Dry petals can also be embedded on a wet sheet of paper through the process of laminating—pressing two layers together.

Be careful when laminating some flower petals, especially rose petals, because they will bleed and stain the paper brown around the petal's edges. Before using any flower petals in your papermaking project, test them for bleeding by sandwiching them between wet paper towels and allowing them

to dry. It will be easy to see if you want that effect on your paper. You can reduce bleeding somewhat by presoaking the petals in warm water for 20 minutes before adding them to the pulp vat for screening. Quick drying the project also helps reduce bleeding.

You can add pieces of gift wrap, tissue paper, colorful paper napkins, and paper doilies during the pulping process. When these papers are pulped in with the other pulp they will be less distinct than if they are added just before screening. You might also want to partially blend these papers and add them to the vat of pulp to produce paper with larger and more noticeable characteristics.

Adding fully pulped tissue paper to the pulp will dye the pulp. Adding partially pulped tissue paper will produce pastel colored paper with darker flecks of color throughout. For a watercolor effect, tear paper napkins and laminate (embed) them on wet pulp.

Snippets of thread and bits of fabric, ribbon, or lace are best added to the pulp just before screening, rather than during pulping because they will become tangled in the blades of the blender. Cut these materials into tiny pieces before adding them to the pulp vat. Experiment with pressing bits of fabric and threads into a wet sheet of paper.

> ### HOT TIP
> *Lavender seeds added to handmade paper will release a wonderful aroma when the paper is torn.*

Part Two:

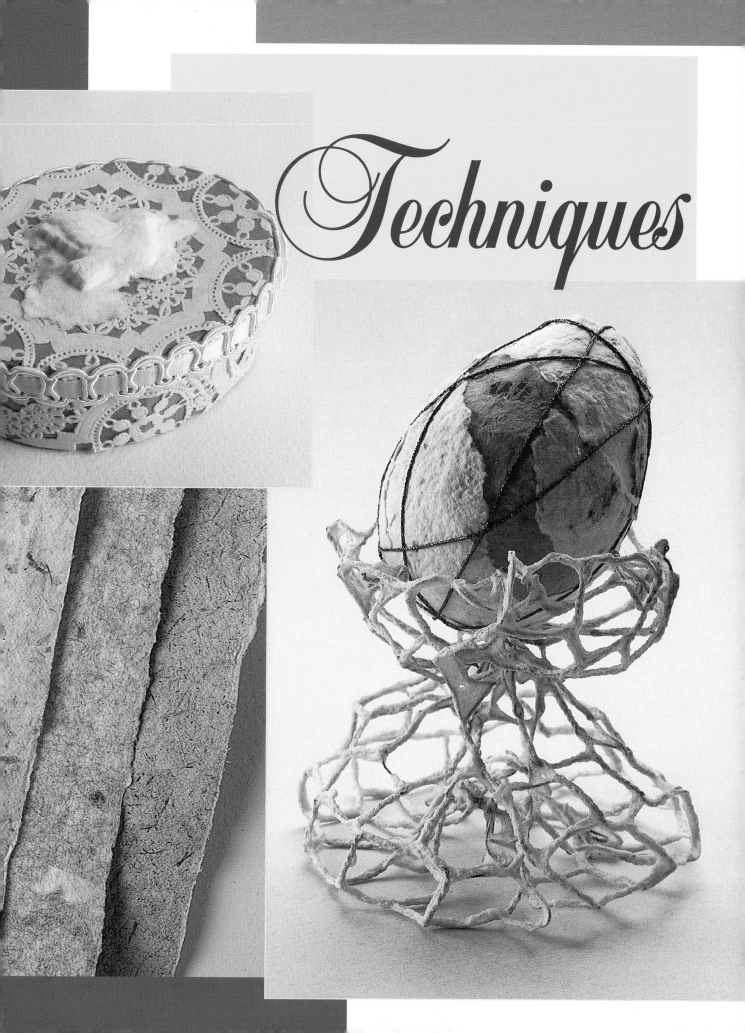

Techniques

The Basics

Pulping

Most paper will break down enough for pulping after soaking in water for several hours. You won't need to cook paper unless it's heavily inked or dirty.

If you are using recycled computer or copier paper, add one part cotton linter to three parts recycled paper to add strength and durability to the handmade paper. Recycled card stock or fine stationery with a high rag content won't require the addition of cotton linter.

When using recycled papers or cotton linter, begin by soaking the materials in water overnight to help break down the fibers. Separate different colors of paper when soaking, as the paper dyes may bleed. Soak heavier paper materials, such as cotton linter, produce cartons, and grocery bags, for several days.

If the recycled paper is heavily inked, smudged or greasy, you may need to cook it first to remove some of the ink and grease. Before cooking, soak the paper overnight and tear it into one-inch pieces. Place it in an old pot, cover it with water and bring to a boil. After it reaches a boil, remove the pot from the heat and allow it to cool. (Be prepared for an obnoxious odor when cooking paper.) Rinse the cooked paper until the water runs clear. The paper is now ready to be pulped.

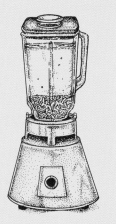

A household blender (or food processor) is necessary for pulping paper.

To begin pulping, put the soaked and torn paper pieces into a blender or food processor and add three parts water for each part paper. Blend on high until the mixture is smooth and creamy—usually one to two minutes, although heavy paper will take longer to blend. For a smoother consistency and finer textured paper, drain the water from the pulp, pour it back into the blender, add three parts water for each part paper and blend more. Always allow the blender or food processor to cool between uses.

Pour the blended pulp into a vat large enough to accommodate your deckle and mold and repeat this process until you have enough pulp for the project you want to complete. Typically, one sheet of handmade paper requires 1½ sheets of recycled paper. It takes about a cup of pulp to make four sheets of 8" x 11" paper. When making several sheets of handmade paper, the vat should be ¾ full with a mixture of approximately 90% water to 10% pulp.

HOT TIP

When starting out, it's easier to manage 5" x 7" sheets of paper. Nearly all the projects are made from this size sheet, even the lampshade on page 90. It really doesn't take much paper to do a project!

For interesting texture and color, add plant fibers, flowers, leaves, bits of tissue paper, gift wrap, or construction paper during the pulping process. Snippets of thread and bits of fabric also add interesting texture and color, but should never be added during blending because the thread and fabric will get tangled in the blender blades. For additional suggestions, refer to the paper recipes at the end of this chapter.

Before making paper with plant material, read the section on natural materials on page 20. Plant fibers should be prepared before beginning the pulping process.

If you plan to make a lot of paper, set up an assembly line, pulping a large quantity of paper at one time. When working with several colors, pulp each color separately and clean the blender thoroughly between colors to prevent residue from one batch of paper pulp from ending up in the next batch.

Paper pulp will keep for one month in the refrigerator or indefinitely in the freezer. Before refrigerating or freezing paper pulp, strain it through a colander positioned over a bucket. Scoop the pulp out of the colander and squeeze out as much water as possible, then place the drained pulp in plastic bags or other containers suitable for the refrigerator or freezer.

Do not pour waste water from straining down the drain, or you'll wind up with a clogged drain. Instead, pour the waste water outside, along the edge of the yard, in an inconspicuous place in the flower bed or in the compost bin. Paper is a natural fiber and will decompose.

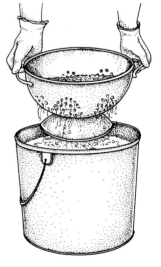

Drain water off the pulp through a colander.

You can also dry the pulp and store it. Just drain it and hang it in a cheesecloth to dry. You can keep dried pulp indefinitely.

Before using refrigerated pulp, it must be reblended with water (90% water, 10% pulp) to a smooth creamy consistency. Frozen pulp should be completely thawed and reblended with water (90/10). Before blending dried pulp, rehydrate it with 90% water to 10% pulp until it's mushy.

Screening

Screening is one way to make sheets of handmade paper. When screening, you simply drag the deckle and mold, screen side up, horizontally through the vat of pulp and water, collecting pulp on the screen as it moves.

If you want to add materials such as glitter, flower petals, leaves, thread snippets, bits of ribbon or lace, do it just before screening. Gently stir the pulp with your hand to bring the paper fibers and bits to the surface.

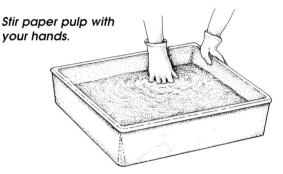

Stir paper pulp with your hands.

Position the deckle on top of the mold with the screen side up. Tightly hold the deckle and mold together with your hands on either side.

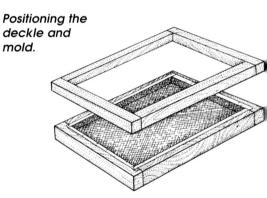

Positioning the deckle and mold.

Dip the deckle and mold into the far end of the vat and pull it toward you in a smooth continuous motion. The deckle and mold enters the vat at a 90 degree angle and as you pull it through the water and pulp, turn it until it's completely submerged horizontally.

Dip the deckle and mold into the far end of the vat.

Hold the deckle and mold at an angle to drain off water.

Lower the deckle and mold into the vat of pulp.

Lift the deckle and mold straight up out of the water and gently shake the pulp from side to side to smooth the pulp and shake off excess water.

Lift the deckle and mold straight up out of the water.

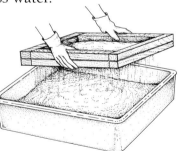

Carefully tilt the deckle and mold at an angle over the vat to drain any additional water from the paper.

HOT TIP
If your hands are dry or sensitive to water, wear gloves during the screening process.

Pouring

You can also make handmade sheets by pouring the pulp onto a deckle that is floating in a vat of water. Both screening and pouring produce beautiful sheets of paper.

Pouring works best when you want to make just a few sheets of paper. When pouring, you fill up a vat with water and make up any amount of pulp you want. For example, if you want to make only one or two sheets, you only need to prepare a small amount of pulp.

Pouring is a great way to experiment with pulp, adding different ingredients for each sheet to see what effect you like best.

When screening, on the other hand, you need at least two blenders full of pulp in the vat along with the water to make it work. Using up all the pulp will produce numerous sheets of paper. Screening works best for "production line" sheet making.

For pouring, the deckle should be approximately two inches deep. A deckle and mold of this type can be purchased or you can make one using the directions on page 14 and substituting 2"-wide boards for the four stretcher bars in the deckle.

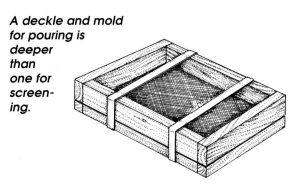

A deckle and mold for pouring is deeper than one for screening.

The pouring deckle and mold floats in the vat and you pour pulp onto it.

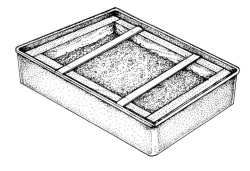

Clamp the deckle and mold together by stretching large rubber bands around both pieces. Fill the vat with enough water to float the deckle and mold with about an inch of water above the screen of the mold. Place the rubber banded deckle and mold screen side up in the vat.

Pour the pulp directly onto the screen inside the deckle and mold. Because the screen is submerged in water, the pulp will spread out and float approximately one inch above it. Gently shake the deckle and mold as you lift it straight up out of the water to smooth the pulp and remove excess water. Carefully tilt the deckle and

mold at an angle over the vat to drain any additional water from the paper. You can change the color and/or texture of the next sheet you pour by using pulp with different ingredients.

You can adapt the pouring method to create cookie cutter designs by positioning the cookie cutter or foam board design on top of the mold and securing it with a rubber band.

You can use a cookie cutter secured on the mold with a rubber band to create shapes.

Balance the mold, cookie cutter side up, across the corner of the vat or over another container to catch the water.

Gently stir the pulp to bring the paper fibers to the top and fill a cup with pulp. Pour the pulp inside the frame of the cookie cutter. Holding the cookie cutter firmly on the mold, gently shake to evenly distribute the pulp. If you want a thicker design, pour more pulp into the cookie cutter, gently shaking each time to evenly distribute the pulp.

Pour paper pulp into the cookie cutter.

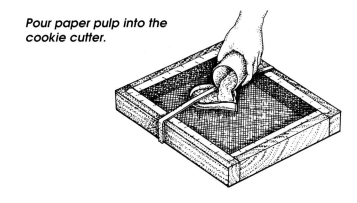

After the water has drained, remove the rubber band and gently lift the cookie cutter straight up from the mold. You can leave the paper pulp on the screen or proceed with the following steps for couching, drying, and sizing.

The alternatives to a deckle and mold are discussed on page 10. A simple pouring device made from a coffee can or plastic container is an inexpensive and fun way to introduce children to the art of papermaking.

You can use the same cookie cutter procedure described above with a plastic lid frame on a container. Don't shake it though, because the pulp will spill off the container. Allow the pulp to dry on the screen. After the pulp has dried, pour the water collected in the container back into the vat of pulp.

Couching

Couching refers to transferring a sheet of newly made paper from the mold to a felt or other surface. When you lift the deckle up off the mold, the mold will be covered with paper pulp. To remove this pulp from the mold, carefully turn the mold over, pulp side down, onto a piece of felt. Sponge the back of the screen to remove additional water.

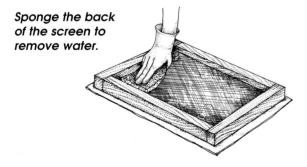

Sponge the back of the screen to remove water.

Starting at one corner of the mold, ease the mold away from the sheet of paper, leaving the paper on the felt.

Lift the mold from the pulp, leaving a sheet of wet paper on the felt.

To join the fibers and squeeze out more water, sandwich the paper pulp between felts, and press with a rolling pin or between two boards. Turn the sandwich over and roll or press again. Carefully remove the top felt and place the sheet of paper and bottom felt on a smooth surface to dry. If the sheet is unsatisfactory, return it to the pulp vat and start over.

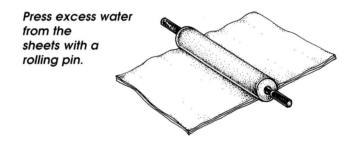

Press excess water from the sheets with a rolling pin.

To make a thicker sheet of paper, couch one sheet of paper on top of another sheet and press them together. This process is referred to as laminating. You can also laminate two different color sheets of paper together or create larger sheets of paper by couching several sheets of paper side by side with overlapping edges, then pressing them together.

If you want a leaf, flower petal, bit of lace or thread to show through the paper, laminate it between two very thin sheets. You can control the thickness of the paper by adjusting the ratio of pulp to water—the less pulp, the thinner the sheet will be.

Couch one thin sheet of paper and place the leaf, grass, petal, or lace on the wet surface. Couch a second thin sheet of pulp on top of the first and use a rolling pin to mesh the fibers together, thus laminating the decoration between the sheets of paper.

To add a flower petal or other decoration on the top of a sheet of paper, carefully position the decoration on a wet sheet of paper right after it's been couched. Use a rolling pin to roll over the decoration, pressing it into the wet paper. The watercolor note cards on page 86 were made in this manner.

You can achieve the effect of embossing or texturing by couching wet paper pulp onto patterned or textured materials, such as corded lace or textured felt. Cover the pulp and use a rolling pin to roll over the pulp, pressing the fabric into the pulp. Leave the lace or felt on the wet paper and allow it to dry on a smooth flat surface. When the pulp has dried completely, carefully pull it away from the dried paper. The design will be embossed into the paper.

Drying

The first thing to remember when you reach the drying stage is to be patient—drying can take several days.

Handmade sheets dry nicely on a flat surface in indirect sunlight or on felts on a flat surface in a warm dry house. Avoid direct sunlight, as it can cause drying paper to fade and curl, especially if you used construction paper to dye the pulp. If drying outdoors, cover the paper with a dry felt to keep any debris from soiling the paper.

For faster drying, place paper sheets between dry felts and iron them with a medium-hot iron, replacing the saturated felts as you go.

Another way to dry paper is to sandwich sheets between felts pressed between two plywood boards that have been treated with waterproof sealant or covered with plastic. First couch the paper onto felts and use a rolling pin to remove as much water from the sheets as possible. Carefully move the wet sheet of paper to a dry felt and stack it on the plywood, adding felts between each layer of paper. Add the top piece of plywood and weight it down with bricks. The actual drying time will depend on the temperature and humidity, but will generally be about a week. To speed up drying and prevent the paper from molding, change the wet felts every two to three days.

If your paper dries wavy or curly, you can flatten it with a medium-hot iron. Always use a pressing cloth both on top and under the paper and be careful not to press too hard or an impression of the iron will appear on the paper. Iron the paper on a smooth, hard surface until flat. Don't iron paper that has been embossed or textured, because the ironing will remove the impressions. You can also flatten sheets between plain white sheets of paper in a flower press or a stack of books.

Dry hand-cast paper and paper sculpture in indirect sunlight outdoors or in a warm dry house. You can also dry these projects in the microwave or conventional oven. For more information about drying hand-cast projects, turn to page 36.

Remember that the texture of the drying surface will be imprinted on your handmade paper. If the pulp dries on a textured surface, such as a towel, embossed felt, or corded lace fabric, the texture of the drying surface will be embossed into the paper.

Before using any surface for drying, test

it to make sure the paper won't permanently stick to it. You may have to treat the surface with nonstick spray. Fabrics such as corded lace can usually be removed by gently pulling the lace away from the dried paper.

minimal pressure to avoid damaging the paper surface.

Test the paper for bleeding in an inconspicuous spot. If the paint or ink still bleeds, apply another coat of sizing to the paper.

Sizing

If you plan to write or paint on your handmade paper, it's a good idea to add sizing to seal the paper surface and prevent the ink or paint from running or bleeding along the lines of fiber. There are a few ways to add sizing to handmade paper, but all of them call for the basic recipe of ½ packet of unflavored gelatin dissolved in ¼ cup of warm water; or one tablespoon of laundry starch mixed in ¼ cup of warm water.

The easiest way to add sizing is to add it to the pulp vat just before using it. Just add ¼ cup of the sizing mixture for every two gallons of vat water.

If you didn't add sizing before screening, you can add it to paper that has dried and cured for at least three weeks by dipping the paper into a shallow tray of sizing mixture. Be careful when handling damp sheets, as they become extremely fragile.

You can also spray the sizing mixture on dried and cured paper sheets. Spray the sizing evenly over each sheet of paper and allow to dry. You may need to thin the mixture a little to prevent the nozzle from clogging.

Finally, you can apply sizing with a soft paint brush, gently spreading it evenly on each sheet of dried and cured paper. Painting allows you to apply a thicker coat of sizing, which is particularly important for calligraphy inks. Use a soft brush and

Clean Up

Empty the vat by straining the pulp through a colander, strainer, or cheesecloth. Repeat this several times, until all the paper pulp is collected. Remove the pulp, squeezing out as much water as possible. You can keep the pulp for up to a month in the refrigerator or indefinitely in the freezer.

Thoroughly wash and rinse all the equipment to remove any residue of paper pulp. If you used kitchen utensils, be sure to clean them very carefully before using them in the kitchen.

Remember, don't pour waste water down the drain, or you're sure to end up with clogged drains. Instead, pour it outside, along the edge of the yard, in an inconspicuous place in the flower bed, or in the compost bin. Paper is a natural fiber and will decompose.

Hand-Casting

Hand-cast paper projects are a great way to embellish cards, bags, and boxes, or as ornaments, frames, and potpourri holders.

You can hand-cast paper pulp into just about any type of mold (for more information on different types of molds, turn to Equipment, page 11.) Remember that paper pulp cast in a very detailed mold won't show all the detail unless it's been finely pulped to a smooth consistency and firmly pressed into the mold.

Pulping for Hand-Casting

Follow the pulping instructions for handmade sheets. It's a good idea to use cotton linter for hand-cast paper projects because recycled paper may not be strong or fine-textured enough to produce the details that add so much to hand-cast paper.

For a smooth glossy finish add kaolin powder to the paper pulp. Follow the manufacturer's directions to determine how much you need. Kaolin powder is usually included in papermaking kits or can be purchased from art suppliers. It's not absolutely necessary to use kaolin to achieve satisfactory results. Without it, the hand-cast mold will be softer and have a matte finish.

Casting

First decide which molds you want to use and clean and dry them. If using terra cotta or plastic molds, spray them with nonstick cooking spray on all surfaces that will come in contact with the paper pulp. Before filling the mold with pulp from your blender, pour the pulp into a colander placed over a bucket or vat and press it with your hands to drain off most of the water.

If you are using pulp from a vat, screen the pulp as you would for making sheets. Allow the water to drain, then couch the pulp into the mold. This creates a more uniform thickness. For a thicker hand-cast mold, repeat the preceding step.

After filling the mold with pulp, begin pressing and spreading the pulp into the mold design with your fingers. Press a sponge into the pulp to remove excess water. Continue to use the sponge and your fingers to gently press the pulp into the mold, working the pulp from the center to the outer edge, keeping it an even thickness. Be sure to press out water and air bubbles, as they will mar the finished project.

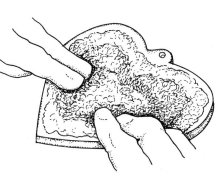

Press pulp into the mold with your fingers.

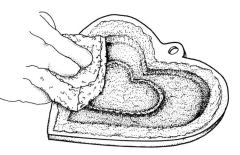

Sponge water from the pulp in the mold.

Allow some of the pulp to spill over the edges of the mold, creating a delicate deckle-edged border. This border will make it easier to remove the dried paper pulp from the mold. Continue to sponge off as much water as possible. This not only reduces the drying time, but it will produce a better impression of the mold.

When working with more than one color, keep each color separate unless you want a mottled appearance. For example, if you're using a flower mold, press the yellow pulp for the center in first, then go on to add pink pulp for the petals and green pulp for the leaves. Avoid pressing the colors into each other or you'll end up with a muddy, indistinct color.

When using a large mold or a plastic candy mold with several small impressions, I find screening a sheet of paper and couching it onto the mold produces good results. Use a sponge and your fingers to gently press the screened pulp into the mold. If there are gaps in the coverage or if you want a thicker mold, cast another sheet of paper and repeat the process as many times as necessary. You can also fill the mold by pouring pulp from the blender, but I sometimes end up with air bubbles in the finished project when I do it this way.

Drying Hand-Casts

Because hand-cast paper is thicker than sheets, it takes longer to dry. However, there are several ways to speed it up. Metal and terra cotta molds can be placed in a preheated 200 degree oven. Turn the oven off before putting the molds in the oven and leave the door open to encourage a warm flow of air to cross over the mold.

You can also use your microwave to dry some terra cotta and clay molds. Check the manufacturer's instructions before using this method. Place the mold in the microwave oven for two minutes on high. Allow the moisture to escape from the microwave by opening the door for one minute, then microwave for another minute. Caution: The molds will be extremely hot, so use hot pads when handling them.

Removing Hand-Cast Paper From the Mold

The pulp should be completely dry before it's removed from the mold. It will take a little longer to dry hand-castings than sheets because they're a little thicker than sheets.

After the pulp has dried completely, use a narrow-blade knife to loosen the edges and lift the hand-cast paper from the mold. The deckle-edged border can be left on or trimmed with scissors. Add the trimmings to your collection of materials for future papermaking projects.

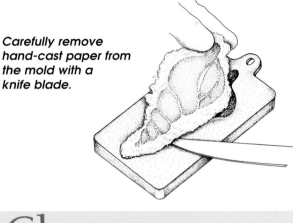

Carefully remove hand-cast paper from the mold with a knife blade.

Clean Up

If you used a vat, empty the vat by straining the pulp through a colander, strainer, or cheesecloth. Repeat this several times, until all the paper pulp is collected. Remove the pulp, squeezing out as much water as possible. You can keep the pulp for up to a month in the refrigerator or indefinitely in the freezer.

Thoroughly wash and rinse all the equipment to remove any residue of paper pulp. If you used kitchen utensils, be sure to clean them very carefully before using them in the kitchen.

Remember, don't pour waste water down the drain, or you're sure to end up with clogged drains. Instead, pour it outside, along the edge of the yard, in an inconspicuous place in the flower bed, or in the compost bin. Paper is a natural fiber and will decompose.

Dip Sculpting

When working with paper pulp, you'll soon discover that the pulp clings to almost anything, which makes for a challenging clean up. But it's because of this clinging quality that you are able to make dipped sculptures with paper pulp.

You can dip all kinds of forms or armatures into the pulp and create interesting effects. Try dipping small wire or plastic baskets, twigs, leaves, or rocks, or create your own wire armature from wire mesh bent into a variety of patterns and shapes.

You can also use floral netting to form an armature. This netting is available at craft and floral stores. Some netting has a plastic coating which must be removed before dipping. If the coating starts to flake off as you bend the netting, remove as much of the coating as possible before dipping it. Just bend and brush it until it's relatively clean.

Any object you dip should be clean and dry. When dipping a wire armature, make sure the wire is rust-free, because rust will bleed through the coats of paper on the form. This isn't necessarily bad, however, because the rust does create an interesting effect and can enrich the character of the sculpture.

Pulping for Dip Sculpting

Follow the instructions on page 42 for preparing the paper pulp using cotton linter. Cotton linter is preferable for dipped sculpture because of the length and strength of the fiber. However, you can use a mixture of cotton linter and recycled papers. You may want to start with a base layer of cotton linter pulp on your armature, then build up layers of recycled paper pulp on top of the cotton linter base.

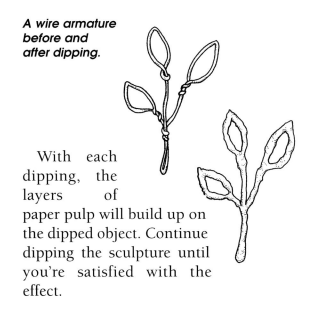

A wire armature before and after dipping.

With each dipping, the layers of paper pulp will build up on the dipped object. Continue dipping the sculpture until you're satisfied with the effect.

Dipping

Ideally, dipping sculpture should be done outdoors because it is very wet and messy. Fill a bucket or vat with enough paper pulp and water to completely submerge the article to be dipped. Experiment with the ratio of pulp to water to achieve the desired appearance. The consistency of the pulp will determine the number of dips required to build up the desired layers of pulp. The best ratio is 90% water to 10% pulp.

Before dipping, gently agitate the pulp with your hand to bring the paper fibers to the surface. Dip the object into the bucket, completely submerging it. After each dipping, allow the pulp to dry.

Drying

You'll need to let each layer of pulp dry on the armature before dipping it again. Dipped sculpture can be propped over a bucket or hung up to dry. Water and pulp will drip from the sculpture, so hang it over a waterproof surface covered with newspaper.

The drying time depends on the thickness and amount of pulp on the sculpture and the temperature and humidity.

You can reduce the drying time for a metal sculpture by placing it in a preheated 200 degree oven. First allow all the water and pulp to drip off the sculpture, then put it in the oven, turn the oven off, and leave the door open to encourage a warm flow of air to cross over the sculpture.

Finishing the Sculpture

After the last layer of pulp has dried completely, seal the sculpture with acrylic sealer. You can further enhance the sculpture with acrylic paints or other ornamentation.

Clean Up

Empty the vat by straining the pulp through a colander, strainer, or cheesecloth. Repeat this several times, until all the paper pulp is collected. Remove the pulp, squeezing out as much water as possible. You can keep the pulp for up to a month in the refrigerator or indefinitely in the freezer.

Thoroughly wash and rinse all the equipment to remove any residue of paper pulp. If you used kitchen utensils, be sure to clean them very carefully before using them in the kitchen.

Remember, don't pour waste water down the drain, or you're sure to end up with clogged drains. Instead, pour it outside, along the edge of the yard, in an inconspicuous place in the flower bed, or in the compost bin. Paper is a natural fiber and will decompose.

Paper Recipes

The following information is presented as "recipes," but they are only suggested combinations. Don't expect your paper to look exactly like the papers used in this book. Each piece of paper from a single vat of pulp will be different—similar but different.

The way you screen the paper, the amount of pulp, the different additives, the way the paper is couched and dried—all play a part in creating each unique sheet of handmade paper. These recipes will provide direction and an idea of what to expect from different combinations of paper and additives.

These recipes use tissue paper and other colored papers to dye the cotton linter, but you can buy cold water dyes to dye paper. Experiment with other additives, such as tempera paint, unsweetened drink mix, food coloring, tea, or coffee. If you do use cold water dyes, wear gloves so you don't discolor your hands.

Refer to the section on Materials for ideas for additives. Keep your eyes open for other things to try. Use your imagination.

Basic Paper Pulp

YOU WILL NEED:
White cotton linter sheets
Water (three parts water to one part cotton linter)
Vat

1. Tear the cotton linter sheets into small pieces and soak them in water until they are soft.

2. Pour the softened cotton linter into a blender or food processor with enough water to cover it, and blend until smooth and creamy.

Cotton linter, which is available at craft stores, is a good strong base for any paper pulp. You can use cotton linter pulp by itself, or combine it with recycled paper or natural materials to create different effects.

The amount of blending and the amount of water in the pulp will affect the texture and look of the finished handmade paper. The more blending, the finer the texture. The more water, the thinner the sheet. The best ratio is 90% water to 10% pulp. If you add too much water, the sheet will spread so thin it will be difficult to get off the screen.

Generally, one 7" x 9" sheet of cotton linter will produce two 8" x 11" sheets of handmade paper. Adding recycled paper to the pulp increases the volume and will produce more sheets of handmade paper.

Pink Tissue Paper

This pulp is dyed and embellished with hot pink tissue paper. For a spattered effect, partially blend pink tissue paper and pour it into the pulp just before screening. To see an example of Pink Tissue paper, turn to the Pressed Flower and Stitched Frame on page 78.

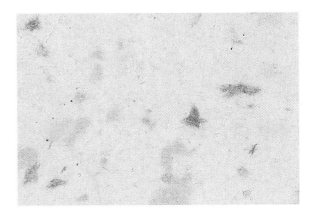

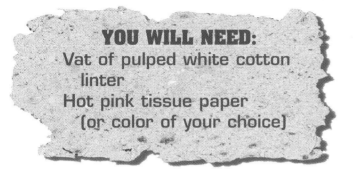

YOU WILL NEED:
Vat of pulped white cotton
    linter
Hot pink tissue paper
    (or color of your choice)

1. Thoroughly pulp and mix a vat of cotton linter.

2. Tear a six-inch square of tissue paper into one-inch pieces and place in the blender. Add enough water to cover the tissue paper and lightly blend. To achieve a spattered look, the tissue paper should be blended except for tiny bits the size of hole punches or smaller. For a smoother, more even color, blend the paper until it is completely pulped or blend and then strain the paper, using only the dyed water to color the white pulp.

3. Pour the blended tissue paper mixture into the vat of cotton linter.

4. Very gently stir the pulp to lightly mix the blended tissue paper into the cotton linter pulp.

5. Screen a sheet of paper.

You can darken the pulp by repeating the process beginning with step two. If the color is too dark, add more cotton linter. With each screening and addition of tissue paper and water, the pulp will be reduced, resulting in thinner sheets of paper

Black & White Tweed Paper

Add black paper to cotton linter to create a tweed effect. If you don't thoroughly blend the black paper into the cotton linter, leaving it a little lumpy, the texture will be a little rougher and more interesting.

This mottled paper is used in the bookmark (page 57), wall pocket (page 59), and collage tray (page 67). The same vat of pulp produced different looks because I varied the amount of cotton linter in the mixture before screening.

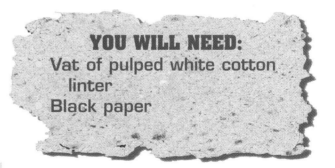

YOU WILL NEED:
Vat of pulped white cotton
    linter
Black paper

1. Lightly pulp and mix a vat of white cotton linter. To achieve a textured look, leave the pulp a little lumpy. This paper will not be suitable for writing or printing.

2. Tear an 8" x 11" sheet of black paper into one-inch pieces and place them in the blender. Add enough water to cover the paper and lightly blend. The black paper should be only partially blended, leaving bits of black paper to be embedded in the cotton linter.

3. Pour the blended black paper mixture into the vat of cotton linter.

4. Very gently stir the pulp to lightly mix the blended black paper into the cotton linter.

5. Screen a sheet of paper.

You can darken the pulp by repeating the process beginning with step two. If the color is too dark, add more cotton linter. For a smoother surface on the paper, blend the cotton linter thoroughly. For a smooth even color, blend some cotton linter and black paper until smooth, then add to the cotton linter pulp. This will result in a gray tone paper.

Gold Flecked White Paper

YOU WILL NEED:
Vat of pulped white cotton linter
Gold foil lace doilies

On close examination, you can see the golden flecks in this paper used to make the Golden Squares Jewelry on page 76. This pulp was also the base for the paper used to make the Rose Petal Book on page 74. The flecks are bits of gold foil lace doilies saved from a previous project.

1. Thoroughly pulp and mix a vat of cotton linter.

2. Punch, cut, or tear several gold foil lace doilies into tiny pieces, hole-punch size or smaller. These doilies will not blend.

3. Scatter the bits of doily in the pulp.

4. Very gently stir the pulp to lightly mix the doily bits with the cotton linter pulp.

5. Screen a sheet of paper.

If you like, add more doily bits as you use the pulp or experiment with other types of decorative papers.

Rose Petal & Gold Paper

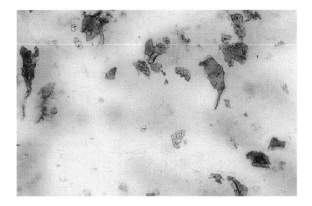

For a different look, add a few crushed rose petals to the Gold Flecked White paper pulp. The reddish-tan spots are caused by the rose petals bleeding into the pulp as the paper dries.

Test flower petals and other foliage for bleeding before using them with paper. Sometimes the bleeding adds interest to the paper, as the rose petals did on this paper, but some petals will bleed and turn dark and ruin the paper. To see an example of this paper, turn to the Rose Petal Book on page 74.

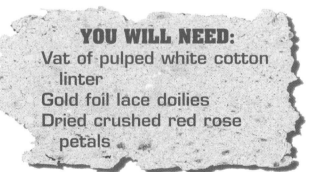

YOU WILL NEED:
Vat of pulped white cotton
    linter
Gold foil lace doilies
Dried crushed red rose
    petals

1. Thoroughly pulp and mix a vat of cotton linter.

2. Punch, cut, or tear several gold doilies into tiny pieces, hole-punch size or smaller. These doilies will not blend.

3. Scatter the bits of doily and dried rose petals in the pulp.

4. Very gently stir the pulp to lightly mix the doily bits and rose petals with the cotton linter pulp.

5. Screen a sheet of paper.

White Paper with Purple Bits

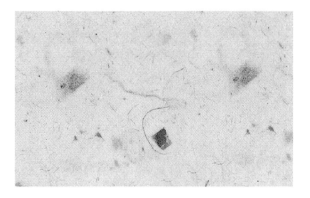

The white triangles on the Purple Triangle Jewelry (page 84) are made from white cotton linter with bits of purple ribbon, thread, and tissue. Save the end pieces of pretty gift wrap ribbon, snippets of threads from stitching projects, and colored tissue paper to use in your papermaking.

YOU WILL NEED:
Vat of pulped white cotton
    linter
Bits of purple gift wrap
    ribbon
Snippets of purple and
    lavender threads
Torn bits of lavender
    tissue paper

1. Thoroughly pulp and mix a vat of cotton linter.

2. Cut purple ribbon into ¼" pieces or smaller.

3. Cut thread snippets into 1" lengths or shorter.

4. Tear the tissue paper into tiny bits—about hole-punch size.

5. Scatter the bits of ribbon, threads, and tissue paper in the pulp and very gently stir the pulp to lightly mix the bits into the cotton linter pulp. Add a few bits at a time until you are happy with the mixture of color and white pulp.

6. Screen a sheet of paper.

If the gift wrap ribbon is not well embedded into the paper, it may flake loose from the dried paper. To prevent the ribbon bits from coming off the paper, paint the finished dried paper with thinned white craft glue to seal. The surface will be a bit harder and slicker than unsealed paper, but you can still write on it.

White & Purple Mottled Paper

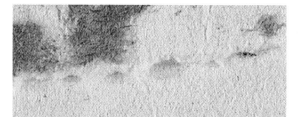

To get this mottled look, add a soaked and pulped purple produce carton to a vat of white cotton linter. Variations of this paper were used to create the Lamp Base and Lampshade on page 90 and the Lavender Potpourri Heart on page 80.

YOU WILL NEED:
Vat of pulped white cotton linter
Purple produce carton, soaked and torn into one-inch pieces

1. Thoroughly pulp a vat of cotton linter.

2. Thoroughly pulp a purple produce carton.

3. Add just a little purple pulp to the white pulp in the vat.

4. Stir the pulp just enough to bring the fibers to the top and achieve a swirled look.

5. Screen a sheet of paper.

Each time you stir the pulp it will blend more, gradually turning a lavender color. You can continue to add purple pulp, making lavender and purple mottled sheets. If you don't have purple produce cartons, try using purple card stock or construction paper.

Purple & White Laminated Paper

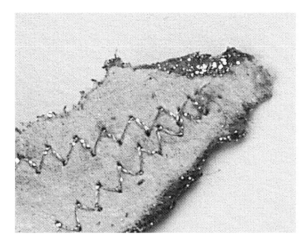

one-inch pieces and place in the blender. Add enough water to cover the tissue paper, blend, and then strain the paper, using only the dyed water to color the white pulp.

3. Couch the purple paper on top of the white paper. Note: The darker color may bleed through to the white side a little.

4. Press between felts with a rolling pin to mesh the fibers together.

5. Allow to dry.

When tearing laminated paper, remember that the color positioned away from you will show on the torn edges.

Laminated paper is created by couching two sheets of paper, one on top of the other, and pressing them together to form one sheet of paper. Both the Gold Stitched Stars Card (page 72) and the Stitched Star Ornament (page 73) are made from laminated paper. These instructions are written for making only one sheet of paper. To make several sheets of paper, you'll need two vats of pulp, one of each color.

Crayon Confetti Paper

YOU WILL NEED:
1½ sheets of white or cream stationery or computer paper
1½ sheets of purple construction paper or white paper pulp dyed with purple tissue paper

1. Pulp, pour, and couch one sheet of white paper.

2. Pulp and pour one sheet of purple paper. Or, if you choose to use dyed white paper pulp, tear a six-inch square of purple tissue paper into

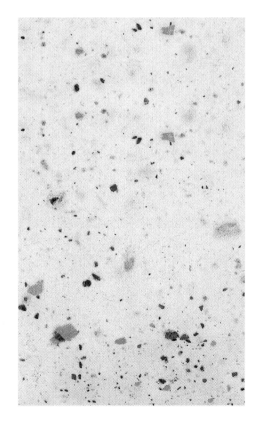

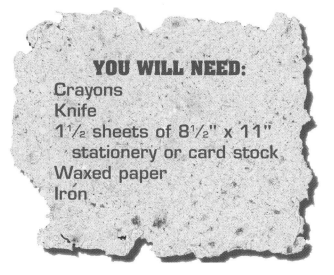

This wonderful effect is the result of adding crayon shavings to a vat of pale pink card stock pulp. By ironing the dried handmade paper, you melt the crayon shavings and disperse the color into the paper. This paper is used to make the Confetti Note Card, Gift Tag, and Bookmark on pages 63-65.

1. Carefully use a knife to shave off bits of crayons.

2. Pulp the stationery or card stock.

3. Pour one sheet of paper.

4. Scatter bits of crayon shavings on the pulp before lifting it out of the vat of water.

5. After the sheet of paper has dried completely, place it between two sheets of waxed paper and iron with a warm iron until the crayon shavings are melted.

Experimenting with plant fibers can yield some surprising results, as was the case with this Iris Leaf paper. You may think you've made a terrible mistake when you first look at the cooked iris leaves, but don't throw them out, because the resulting paper is beautifully translucent.

Because this paper is more difficult to make, you'll want to use it sparingly, embellishing other projects with pieces of it, as you can see on the Raffia Bookmark (page 66), Raffia and Leaf Gift Tag (page 61), and the Floral Card (page 69).

Iris Leaf Paper

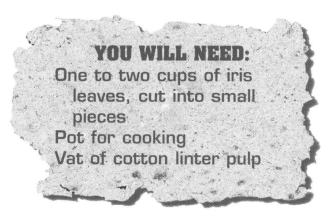

1. Cook cut-up iris leaves until tender. Be sure the area is well ventilated, as there is an odor when these leaves are cooking. Allow to cool.

2. Pulp iris leaves in a blender. The pulp will be stringy, but the strings will add interest to the finished paper.

3. Add some cotton linter pulp to the pulped iris leaves at a ratio of half and half and blend.

Cotton linter adds strength to the paper and doubles the amount of paper you can make. You can also make paper from pure iris leaf pulp if you choose.

4. Pour a sheet of paper.

Experiment with local plant fibers and document the results for future use. I've made some lovely and interesting papers with okra, onion skins, and garlic skins.

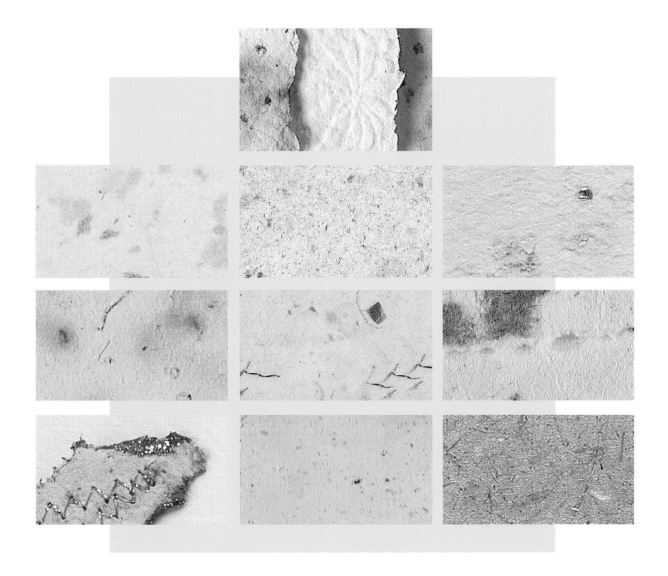

Some of the projects that follow are simple, others are a little more involved. Each of them is made from a paper recipe in this book with techniques that are fully explained.

Many of the papers and methods used in creating the easier projects—cards, gift tags, and bookmarks—are combined and incorporated to create some of the larger and more detailed projects. They all begin with the basic paper pulp.

Read both the general instructions that follow and the project instructions before beginning.

Part Three:

Projects

General Instructions

Tools

You probably already own most of the tools necessary to complete the projects in this book. The list includes a straight edge ruler, a craft knife, scissors, pinking shears, a hole punch, an awl or ice pick, a chenille needle, a tapestry needle, and a sewing machine with a zigzag stitch.

Soft paint brushes in various sizes are necessary to apply sizing, paint, and diluted white craft glue. A stencil brush works best to paint raised designs, such as on the Rose Petal Potpourri Heart on page 104.

Cutting and Tearing Paper

For a hard straight edge, cut handmade paper with scissors or a craft knife. If you prefer a rough deckle-look edge, tear the paper against and along the straight edge of a ruler.

You can tear paper using a straight edge ruler as a guide.

Using pinking shears instead of scissors creates an interesting and decorative edge. Experiment with other decorative edge scissors to create scallops or other edgings to complement the softness of handmade paper.

Patterns

Trace a pattern shape onto stiff cardboard and cut out the shape with a craft knife. Place the cardboard pattern on top of the handmade paper and hold it securely with one hand. Carefully pull the handmade paper up against the cardboard, applying enough pressure to tear the paper.

You can tear paper with a cardboard pattern.

When pulling the paper toward you, the color on

the back side will show along the ragged edges. Keep this in mind when working with laminated paper in contrasting colors.

The dark laminated paper on the bottom shows on the torn edges.

Gluing

Before using any glue, do a test by applying the glue on scraps of paper to make sure it won't seep into the paper and leave unsightly spots. Some glues, such as rubber cement, library paste, glue sticks and clear brown glues may be too sticky and cause bits of the fragile handmade paper to tear away as the glue is applied.

Experiment with different glues before beginning a project. Remember that handmade paper is very porous and many glues will soak into it. If this happens, the glue loses its stickiness and may cause unsightly spots on the right side of the paper.

The surface of the paper will expand somewhat when you apply glue to it. As the glue dries, the surface contracts, sometimes causing waves on the surface of the paper. To avoid this, apply light thin coats or very small amounts, thus preventing the surface from getting too wet.

White craft glue works well with handmade paper. In small areas, use toothpicks to dab a tiny spot of glue on the paper. For larger areas, dilute white craft glue with water until it's a good painting consistency and paint it on with a brush.

You can also use diluted white craft glue to attach and seal foliage to handmade paper projects.

Fabric glue also works well with handmade paper, probably due to the high content of cotton fibers in the paper. Experiment with different fabric glues to find the one that works best for your project.

If you must use "super glue," apply small amounts to very small areas and remember that you can't change your mind once the glue has set.

If you are adept with a glue gun, you can certainly use one with paper. Apply only very thin lines of hot glue. If you can't control the gun adequately to produce only thin lines, don't use it, as too much glue on the paper will ruin it.

Remember that once any glue has been applied to handmade paper, the paper is no longer suitable to save for use in other papermaking projects.

Hand-Stitching

Since I have an extensive sewing background, I often treat handmade paper as fine fabric, stitching it by hand or with the sewing machine.

Any time you puncture paper, the holes

will show, so be sure to accurately mark the stitching before beginning. If you change your mind after stitching the paper, dampen it with a sponge along the stitching line and gently press to close the needle holes. This won't always close the holes, but it's worth a try. If the holes are too big to close, you'll have to add this piece of paper to your scrap bin to be used in the next batch of pulp.

Avoid closely spaced stitching, which is more likely to cause the paper to tear. Instead, use stitching with wide spacing, such as running stitches or blanket stitches.

You can use both chenille and tapestry needles for hand-stitching paper projects. Select a sharp-pointed chenille needle to stitch the paper with decorative threads and a dull-pointed tapestry needle to lace ribbons, thread, and raffia.

Most needlework and hand-sewing threads work fine with paper. Some yarn or heavy crewel threads may be too large and cause the paper to tear.

Before hand-stitching especially fragile paper, reinforce the paper by laying it on top of a piece of card stock and stitching through both layers. Lightweight iron-on interfacing also provides excellent reinforcement. Follow the manufacturer's directions to apply the interfacing on the back side of the paper project.

You can also reinforce paper with fabric by applying iron-on adhesive between the paper and the fabric. Just follow the manufacturer's instructions to apply the adhesive to the fabric and the fabric to the handmade paper.

Machine-Stitching

When using your sewing machine to stitch handmade paper, make sure your machine needle is new and sharp. Paper is much more fragile than fabric, so a dull needle will almost certainly tear it.

As with hand-stitching, a closely spaced straight running stitch is likely to cause the paper to tear. Instead, use a long wide zigzag stitch and reinforce thin or extremely fragile paper before stitching it. You can also use a zigzag stitch to make a decorative accent or to combine small sheets of handmade paper into a larger collage of sheets.

When machine-stitching paper, always place the paper right side up, with the reinforcement on the back side. It is the feed of your machine that will most likely tear the paper, especially if the paper has a rough texture.

If you reinforce the paper by laying it on card stock, make sure your sewing machine can handle stitching through both layers. Always use a new, sharp sewing needle and adjust the thread tension and pressure foot as needed. The paper should move smoothly without pulling under the pressure foot. After you have determined that your sewing machine will sew on card stock, do a test on some samples of the handmade paper you plan to use in your project. If the paper has a rough texture, it may catch on the pressure foot or tear easily when the needle punctures the paper.

Most machine sewing threads are acceptable for stitching paper. Experiment with quilting threads and metallic sewing threads to add interest to your projects.

For lacing with ribbon or cording, use a hole punch to create large holes. An awl or ice pick is ideal for making smaller holes for finer lacing.

Sheet Projects

ards, gift tags, and bookmarks are easy projects and most can be completed in 30 minutes. These are great projects to share with children because the children can do most of the steps themselves. (Always keep sharp scissors and craft knives away from children.)

Customize these projects for a particular person or special occasion by changing the type of paper and embellishments.

Velvet Ribbon Bookmark

$\mathcal{S}$imple but elegant, this bookmark is a wonderful gift for a special reader in your life. The black velvet ribbon showcases the beautiful texture and mottled color of the handmade paper.

YOU WILL NEED:
5" x 10" sheet of Black and White Tweed handmade paper (Find the recipe on page 43.)
12" length of ¹/₂"-wide black velvet ribbon
Straight edge ruler
Craft knife
Scissors

1. Mark the sheet of Black and White Tweed paper to measure 1½" x 7" and use the straight edge of a ruler to tear it.

2. Measure and mark the position of the slits at approximately 1" intervals. Carefully cut out ½" slits with a craft knife.

3. Thread the ribbon through the slits, leaving approximately 2½" of ribbon on either end.

Thread the ribbon through the slits in the bookmark.

4. Use scissors to cut dovetails in the ribbon ends approximately 1" from the end of the bookmark.

Stitched Wall Pocket

For an added decorative touch, cut out the fabric pieces with pinking shears. The fabric not only looks great, it adds strength to the paper as well. The button straps looped over the hanger create a whimsical, country look and you can use the pocket to hold a tiny bouquet of dried flowers.

YOU WILL NEED:
- 2 5" x 7" pieces of Black and White Tweed handmade paper (Find the recipe on page 43.)
- 12" square of cotton fabric in a black print
- 12" square of iron-on fabric adhesive
- 12" length of ⅝"-wide black velvet ribbon
- Red sewing machine thread
- Black sewing thread
- 2 ½"-diameter red 4-hole buttons
- Sewing needle
- Pinking shears
- Scissors
- Sewing machine with zigzag stitch
- White craft glue
- Decorative 8" black metal hanger (I found one with a star design.)

1. Follow the manufacturer's instructions to apply iron-on fabric adhesive to the back of the 12" square of fabric.

2. Using pinking shears, cut two 4½" x 6" pieces from the fabric.

3. Center one of the fabric pieces on each piece of handmade paper and follow the adhesive manufacturer's directions to join the fabric to the paper.

Iron the fabric onto the handmade paper.

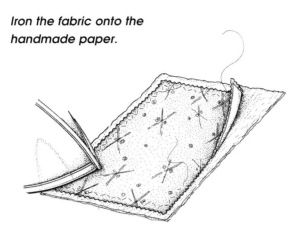

4. Thread your sewing machine with red sewing thread and zigzag stitch on both sheets, approximately ½" in from the fabric edge, through the fabric and paper.

5. Create the pocket flap by making a 2½" fold on the vertical of one of the sheets.

The folded flap and back view of the wall pocket.

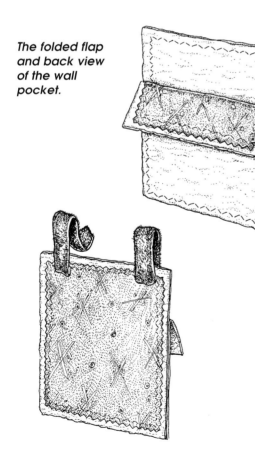

6. Place the unfolded sheet on a flat surface with the fabric side down. Place the folded sheet, fabric side down, on top of the unfolded sheet. The fabric flap should show on the outside of the pocket. Match the bottom edges and sides of both sheets and glue them together along the bottom edges and sides. Allow to dry.

7. Cut the ribbon in half and cut points at one end of each ribbon piece.

8. Use black thread to sew the buttons on the pointed ends of each ribbon piece.

9. Glue the ribbon ends with the buttons at the top of the paper pocket. Allow to dry.

Place the ribbons and buttons as shown.

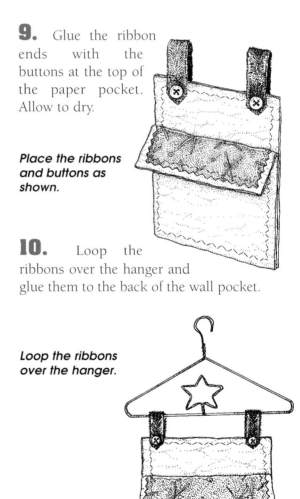

10. Loop the ribbons over the hanger and glue them to the back of the wall pocket.

Loop the ribbons over the hanger.

Raffia & Leaf Gift Tag

YOU WILL NEED:
Scrap of Iris Leaf paper (Find
   the recipe on page 48.)
2" x 3" cream-colored card
   stock
18" length of raffia
Pieces of pressed and dried
   foliage
Craft knife or scissors
Chenille needle
White craft glue
Paint brush for glue
Hole punch

This gift tag is made from Iris Leaf paper, but don't feel limited to this type of paper. Experiment using other papers and dried foliage.

1. Using the straight edge of a ruler as a tearing guide, tear a piece of Iris Leaf paper ¼" smaller than the 2" x 3" card (1¾" x 2¾").

2. Thread a chenille needle with a piece of raffia. Hand-stitch a running stitch approximately ¼" from the edge of the Iris Leaf paper.

Stitch around the card with raffia.

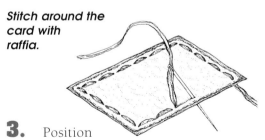

3. Position the pressed leaves on the Iris Leaf paper inside the stitches and glue them in place by brushing thinned glue under and over the pressed leaves. Allow to dry.

4. Glue the piece of Iris Leaf paper on the cream-colored card. Allow to dry.

5. Using a hole punch, punch a hole in the corner of the card.

6. Thread raffia through the hole and tie.

Confetti Creations

This is fun! When working with handmade paper and crayon shavings, there is a wonderful element of surprise. It's always interesting to see how the look of the paper changes after the crayon shavings have melted. What a great way to use all those old broken crayons, not to mention those too-short lengths of leftover gift wrap ribbon.

Confetti
Bookmark

YOU WILL NEED:
5" x 10" or larger sheet
of handmade paper
Crayon shavings of
mixed colors (the
smallest bits possible)
2 12" lengths of curling
ribbon in coordinating
colors
Straight edge ruler
Hole punch

1. Sprinkle the crayon bits on a sheet of handmade paper and sandwich the paper between two sheets of waxed paper. Press with a warm iron until the crayon bits are melted.

2. Mark the paper with the measurements for a 1½" x 7" bookmark. Using the straight edge of a ruler as a guide, tear the bookmark from the paper along the edge of the ruler.

3. Measure and mark the position of ten ribbon holes, approximately every ¾". Using a hole punch, punch holes in the bookmark at the marks.

4. Thread both lengths of ribbon through the holes, leaving approximately 2½" of ribbon on either end.

Thread ribbon through the holes in the bookmark.

5. Curl the ribbon ends with the straight edge of a scissors.

Confetti Gift Tag

*A*fter making the bookmark, use the remaining paper to make gift tags. Each project will look a little different, depending on the color of the crayons you melt in the paper.

YOU WILL NEED:
Handmade paper
Crayon shavings of mixed
    colors (the smallest
    bits possible)
2 6" lengths of curling
    ribbon in coordinating
    colors
Straight edge ruler
Stencil (optional)
Wide marker in a
    coordinating color
Fine black marker
Plain paper in a
    coordinating color
Craft knife or scissors
White craft glue
Hole punch

1. Sprinkle the crayon bits on a sheet of handmade paper and sandwich the paper between two sheets of waxed paper. Press with a warm iron until the crayon bits are melted.

2. Mark the paper with the measurement for a 2" x 3" gift tag. Using the straight edge of a ruler as a guide, tear the paper along the edge of the ruler.

3. Use the wide colored marker to stencil or hand-letter "For You" on the card and outline the lettering with fine black marker.

4. Measure and cut a plain sheet of paper approximately ¼" smaller than the card.

5. Glue the plain sheet of paper to the back of the card.

6. Using a hole punch, punch a hole in the upper left hand corner of the card.

7. Thread both lengths of ribbon through the hole and tie.

8. Curl the ribbon ends with the straight edge of a scissors.

Happy Birthday

Confetti Note Card

The bright festive colors of this paper make a festive birthday card. A get well card in these cheery colors would lift spirits and brighten the sick room.

1. Sprinkle the crayon bits on the sheet of handmade paper and sandwich the paper between two sheets of waxed paper. Press with a warm iron until the crayon bits are melted.

2. Fold the paper in half. Using the wide colored marker, stencil or hand-letter "Happy Birthday" on the front of the card and outline the lettering with fine black marker.

3. Measure and cut a plain sheet of colored paper approximately ½" smaller than the handmade sheet and fold it in half.

4. Glue the plain sheet of colored paper inside the handmade card, along the fold.

5. Using a hole punch, punch a hole in the upper left hand corner of the card.

6. Thread both lengths of ribbon through the hole and tie.

7. Curl the ribbon ends with the straight edge of a scissors.

Raffia Bookmark

The natural texture and color of Iris Leaf paper is shown to best advantage in a muted, subtle setting. Using corrugated cardboard and raffia brings out the special qualities of this paper.

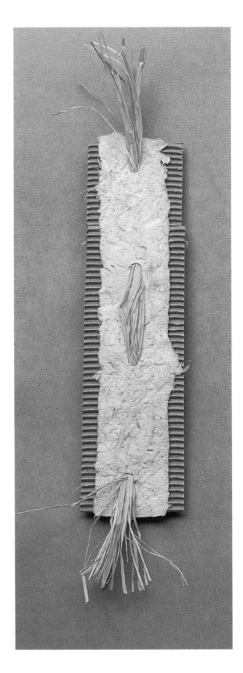

YOU WILL NEED:
- 5" x 10" sheet of handmade Iris Leaf paper (Find the recipe on page 48.)
- 12" length of raffia
- 3" x 8" piece of corrugated cardboard
- Straight edge ruler
- Hole punch
- Craft knife or scissors
- White craft glue

1. Mark the paper with the measurements for a 1½" x 7" bookmark. Using the straight edge of a ruler as a guide, tear the bookmark from the paper along the ruler edge.

2. Measure and mark approximately ½" from either end of the bookmark and again at 2" intervals.

3. Using a hole punch, punch holes at the marks.

4. Carefully thread the raffia through the holes and trim the raffia to approximately 2½" on either end.

5. Measure and cut a 2" x 7" strip of corrugated cardboard.

6. Center the handmade paper bookmark on the corrugated cardboard, aligning the ends, and glue in place.

Paper Collage Tray

*C*reate a one-of-a-kind collage from strips of handmade paper, then line a wooden tray with your creation. Customize it even further by painting the tray to match your decor. You can glue the paper strips together or stitch them, either by hand or with your sewing machine.

YOU WILL NEED:

Variety of handmade papers, torn into strips
Wooden tray
Glass or acrylic cut to fit inside tray
Acrylic paint or sealer (optional)
Heavy paper for pattern
Paint brush
Scissors
Straight edge ruler
White craft glue

1. If desired, finish the wooden tray with acrylic paint or sealer. Allow to dry.

2. Measure the interior dimensions of the tray and cut a pattern from heavy paper.

Assemble the torn paper strips into a pleasing design on the pattern.

Measure the interior dimensions of the tray.

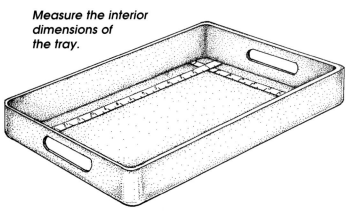

4. Arrange and rearrange the strips on the paper pattern until you are pleased with the collage design.

5. Glue the strips together at the ends and along the edges to form the collage. Allow to dry.

3. Using a straight edge ruler as a guide, tear strips of handmade paper in varying lengths and widths.

6. Carefully lay the paper collage in the bottom of the tray and cover it with the cut-to-size piece of glass or acrylic. (Avoid serving liquids on this tray, as any moisture that collects under the protective glass or acrylic will damage the paper.)

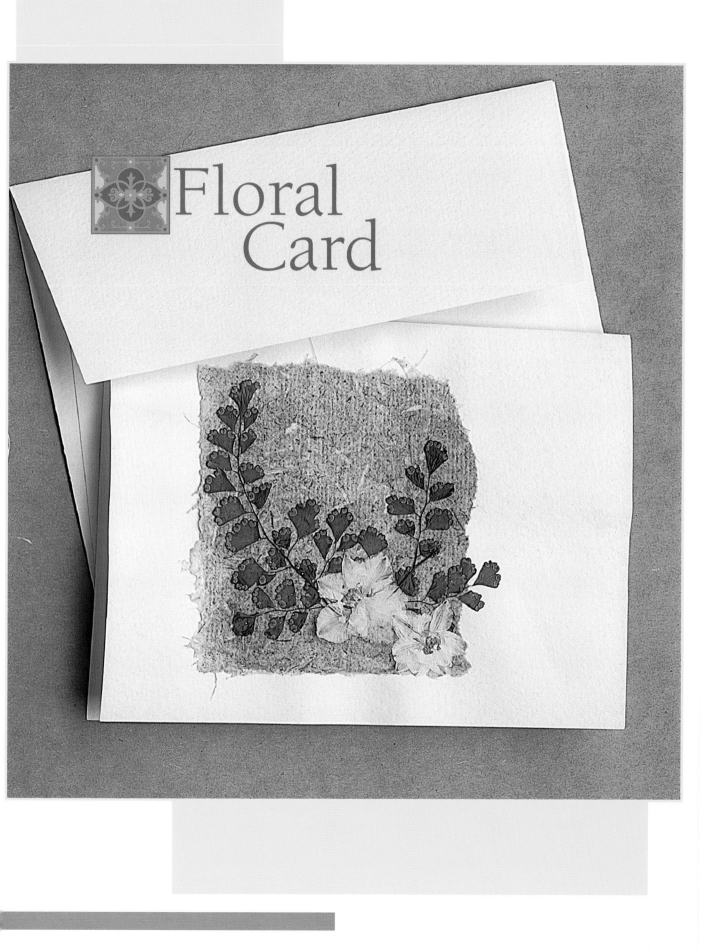

Floral
Card

As you will find, making any natural fiber paper is labor intensive, and Iris Leaf paper is no exception, so a little paper needs to go a long way. This card is a great way to showcase this lovely translucent paper and still have paper left for other projects.

YOU WILL NEED:

5" square of Iris Leaf paper (Find the recipe on page 48.)
5" x 6⅞" blank cream-colored greeting card with envelope
Pieces of pressed and dried foliage
2 pressed and dried white flowers
White craft glue
Paint brush

1. Using the straight edge of a ruler as a tearing guide, tear a 3½" square of Iris Leaf paper.

2. Brush thinned glue on the back of the Iris Leaf paper and glue it on the card.

3. Place the foliage in a pleasing design on the Iris Leaf paper. Brush thinned glue under and over the foliage. Allow to dry.

4. Position the pressed flowers in a pleasing design on top of the foliage. Brush thinned glue under and over the flowers. Allow to dry.

Gold Stitched Star Card & Ornament

This card is made with laminated paper, glitter fabric paint, and gold metallic threads. Laminated paper is stronger than most handmade paper because it is actually two sheets of paper joined together. Laminated paper shouldn't require any additional reinforcement before stitching.

Gold Stitched Star Card

1. Lightly brush gold glitter fabric paint on the front of the card and on the flap of the envelope. Allow to dry.

2. Transfer the star pattern (right) onto a piece of cardboard and cut it out with a craft knife.

3. Place the cardboard pattern on top of the laminated handmade paper. Firmly holding the cardboard pattern with one hand, carefully pull the handmade paper against the cardboard, tearing the star from the handmade paper. By placing the purple side down while tearing, the purple will show along the torn edges.

4. Thread your sewing machine with gold metallic sewing thread and zigzag stitch the star pattern on each star approximately ¼" from the edge of the star.

5. Paint gold glitter fabric paint along the outside edge of the stars.

6. Glue the stars on the front of the card.

The star pattern with the zigzag stitching guideline.

Gold Stitched Star Ornament

*S*titch several star ornaments to coordinate with the Gold Stitched Star Card or make a star garland by stringing a dozen stars on a golden cord.

YOU WILL NEED:
Laminated handmade paper made from one white sheet and one purple sheet (See the directions for laminated paper on page 31.)
Gold metallic sewing thread
8" length of ¼" gold ribbon
Gold glitter fabric paint
Cardboard for pattern
Sewing machine with zigzag stitch
Paint brush
Hole punch

1. Transfer the star pattern from page 72 onto a piece of cardboard and cut it out with a craft knife.

2. Place the pattern on top of the handmade paper. Holding it with one hand, carefully pull the handmade paper against the cardboard, tearing the star from the handmade paper. By placing the purple side down while tearing, the purple will show along the torn edges.

3. Thread your sewing machine with gold metallic sewing thread and zigzag stitch the star

pattern on each star approximately ¼" in from the edge of the star.

4. Paint gold glitter fabric paint along the outside edge of the stars.

5. Use a hole punch to punch a hole in the star.

6. Thread the ribbon through the punched hole and tie.

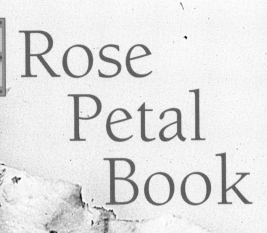

Rose
Petal
Book

For a truly individual guest book, cover it with handmade paper embedded with rose petals and fill it with pretty pink stationery. The raffia bow that holds it together completes the look.

YOU WILL NEED:
2 5" x 7" sheets of Rose Petal and Gold paper (Find the recipe on page 44.)
10 or more sheets of 4" x 6" pink writing paper
3 yards of raffia
Hole punch

1. Cut the pink paper into 4" x 6" sheets. If you'd like to use handmade paper sheets as stationery, you can substitute very smooth-surfaced handmade paper sheets cut to a uniform 4" x 6" size.

2. Sandwich the writing paper between the two sheets of Rose Petal and Gold paper, positioning the paper ½" from the left edge and centering it between the top and bottom edges.

3. Using a hole punch, punch two holes through all layers of paper approximately ½" in from the left edge of the Rose Petal and Gold paper and 1½" from the top and bottom edges.

4. Thread raffia through the holes, tie in a bow, and trim the ends as needed.

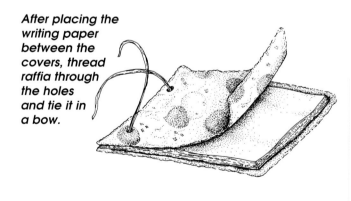

After placing the writing paper between the covers, thread raffia through the holes and tie it in a bow.

Golden Squares Necklace & Earrings

Do you have a heart of gold (from the Golden Hearts Garland on page 94) that is broken? Don't despair. Incorporate the paper from that broken heart into this jewelry. If you didn't make the garland, you can still make your golden squares. Be creative and combine other bits of paper to make this matching set.

YOU WILL NEED:

Scraps of white
   handmade paper
   (scraps of sheets of
   paper will work fine)
Scraps of Gold Flecked
   White handmade paper
   (Find the recipe on
   page 44.)
Gold liquid glitter
1 yard of very fine gold

cord (05 gauge)
Beacon Liquid
   Laminate or Mod
   Podge
2 1" squares of card
   stock
Earring backs
White craft glue
Paint brush

1. Shake the liquid glitter to blend and pour approximately ½" liquid into a shallow container.

2. Carefully dip the scraps of white handmade paper into the glitter, covering both sides. Be careful, the paper will become extremely fragile when wet. If too much glitter collects on the paper, gently dab it off with a paper towel. Place the scraps on waxed paper to dry.

3. Tear two 1½" squares and two ½" squares from the gold-dipped white paper,

4. Tear one 1½" square, four 1" squares and one ½" square from the Gold Flecked White paper.

5. Tear the ½" Gold Flecked White square into an "L" shape.

6. To create the necklace design, glue a ½" Gold Flecked White square and the "L" shape on one of the 1½" gold-dipped squares.

7. To create the earrings, glue a ½" gold-dipped square on each of the 1" Gold Flecked White squares.

8. Paint three coats of liquid laminate on all sides of all the squares, allowing them to dry completely between each coat.

9. For the necklace, glue the two ends of the gold cord on the back of the 1½" embellished square. Position the second gold-dipped 1½" square over the cord, aligning it with the bottom square and covering the ends of the cord. Glue in place.

Glue the cord between the front and back pieces of the necklace.

10. For the earrings, glue a 1" square of card stock on the back of each 1" embellished square and allow to dry. Glue an earring back on the back of each.

Position the squares on the necklace and earrings.

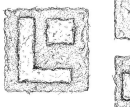

Pressed Flower & Stitched Frame

ried, pressed foliage and a white cord embellish this elegant frame and the zigzag stitching across the mitered corners adds color. You can adapt this design to fit any size frame.

YOU WILL NEED:

Large sheet of handmade
　paper (The paper used
　here is pink with bits of
　hot pink tissue paper.)
Your choice of photo frame
　(Shown here is
　a 9" x 7" papier mâché
　frame.)
1 yard ¼"-wide white satin
　cord

Coordinating thread
4 sprigs of pressed and
　dried foliage
4 pressed and dried
　flowers
Straight edge ruler
Sewing machine with zigzag
　stitch
Paint brush
White craft glue
Scissors

1. Measure the length and width of the frame and transfer the measurements to the sheet of handmade paper.

2. Using the straight edge of a ruler as a guide, tear strips from the handmade paper along the ruler edge to match the measurements of the frame.

3. Position the paper strips on the frame. Determine where to miter the corners, allowing an overlap of ½" at the mitered corners on the top and bottom strips.

Line up the paper strips on the frame and mark the mitered corners.

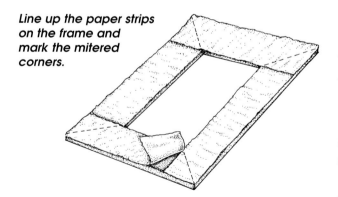

4. Using the straight edge of a ruler as a guide, tear the paper across the corner and along the ruler edge. Allow the corner strips of the short pieces at the top and bottom to overlap approximately ½" for stitching.

5. Position the paper pieces together to form a paper frame, aligning the mitered corners.

6. Zigzag stitch diagonally across each corner.

7. Position the paper frame on top of the photo frame and glue it in place. Allow to dry.

8. Position the foliage on the paper frame. Brush thinned glue under and over the pressed foliage and glue it on the paper frame. Allow to dry.

9. Position the pressed flowers on top of the foliage. Brush thinned glue under and over the pressed flowers and glue them on the foliage. Allow to dry.

10. Glue the white cord along the outside edge of the frame. Overlap the ends of the cord and trim off the excess.

Add cording to the finished frame.

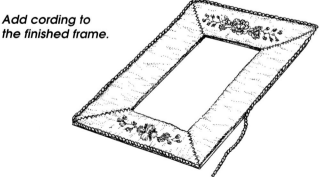

Lavender & Lace Potpourri Heart

The combination of lovely lavender handmade paper with cream-colored lace, a bit of ribbon, and a button, make a beautiful Victorian potpourri heart. Fill the heart with lavender seeds for a sweet smelling lingerie sachet. Make one for each bridesmaid, using a bit of lace and satin from the bride's gown.

YOU WILL NEED:

2 5" squares of lavender handmade paper (This is a variation of the White and Purple Mottled Paper recipe on page 46. I began with white pulp and added a little coarsely blended purple carton, screened a sheet, then a little more, screened another sheet, and so on. Each sheet that's screened will look a little different than the one before it.)

2 5" squares of tulle
2 5" squares of lace (corded or crochet-type)
1 tablespoon lavender seeds
12" length of 1/4"-wide white picot edge ribbon
5/8" white button
Cardboard for pattern
Scissors
White craft glue

1. Transfer the heart pattern onto a piece of cardboard and cut it out with a craft knife.

2. Place the pattern on top of the handmade paper. Firmly hold the cardboard pattern down with one hand while carefully pulling the handmade paper up against it, tearing the heart shape from the handmade paper. Repeat to tear another heart shape.

Cut out the inside of the heart.

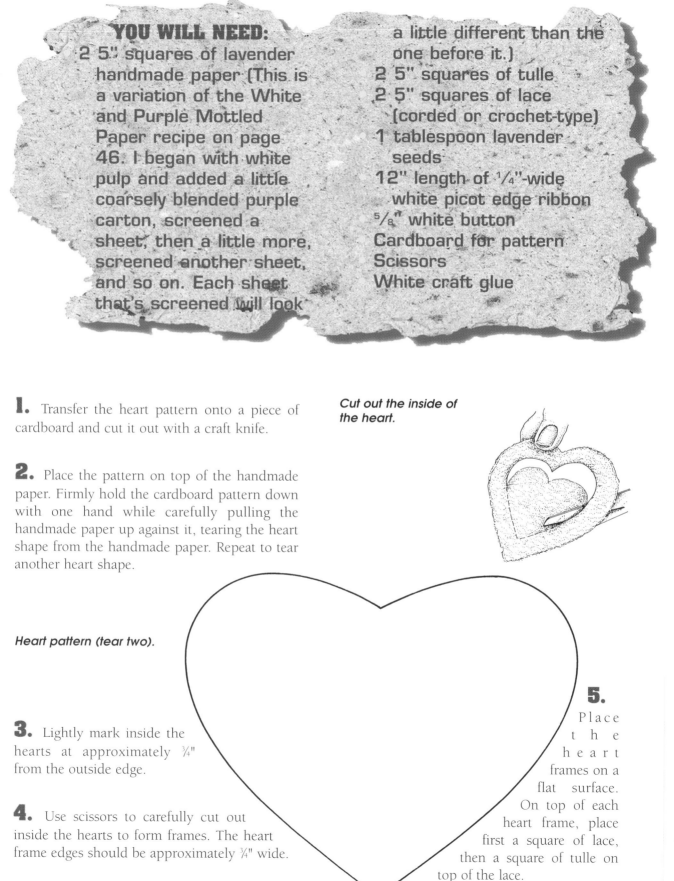

Heart pattern (tear two).

3. Lightly mark inside the hearts at approximately 3/4" from the outside edge.

4. Use scissors to carefully cut out inside the hearts to form frames. The heart frame edges should be approximately 3/4" wide.

5. Place the heart frames on a flat surface. On top of each heart frame, place first a square of lace, then a square of tulle on top of the lace.

Place lace and tulle on the heart frames.

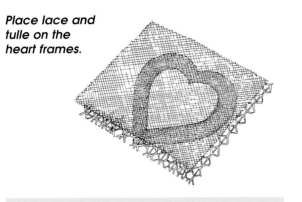

Place lavender seeds in the center on top of the tulle.

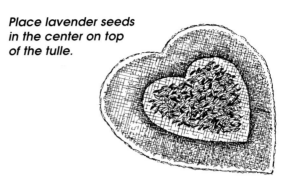

HOT TIP

The tulle is on the inside of the lace to prevent the seeds from slipping through the large openings of the lace. You can substitute any coordinating cotton fabric or lace or use an antique linen handkerchief, some eyelet, or a bit of satin or lace from a bridal gown. Look through your fabric scraps for pieces of fabric to coordinate with the handmade paper hearts.

9. Position the second heart, with tulle to the inside, on top of the heart with lavender seeds. Align the edges of both hearts and glue them together along the inside and outside edges. Allow to dry.

10. Glue the ribbon in a cross at the top center of the heart.

Cross the ribbon at the top of the heart and glue it in place with the button over the cross.

6. Glue the lace and tulle squares along the inside edges of both heart frames. Allow to dry.

7. Use scissors to carefully trim away the overlap of lace and tulle so they don't show along the outside edge of the heart frame.

8. Spoon lavender seeds into the center and on top of the tulle of one heart.

11. Glue the button over the center of the ribbon cross.

Printed Flower Gift Tag

This gift tag is embellished with printing, coloring, and hand-stitching. The design is printed on, then colored in with markers. I used blanket stitching to finish the outside edge. This is a good project for children to help with. They can easily do the printing and coloring and mom can do the stitching.

YOU WILL NEED:
2" x 3" piece of
   handmade paper
Coordinating pearl
   cotton thread
Flower stamp
Stamp pad
Coordinating markers
Craft knife
Chenille needle

1. Using a craft knife or scissors, cut a 2" x 3" card from handmade paper.

2. Stamp the flower design on the center front of the card.

3. Using coordinating markers, fill in the flower design as desired.

4. Thread a chenille needle with coordinating pearl cotton thread. Beginning at one corner, blanket stitch around the card, ending with a 6" tail of thread. Tie off the thread ends.

Blanket stitch around the gift tag.

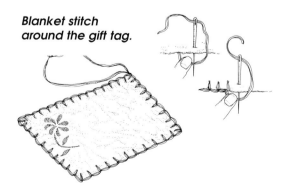

Purple Triangle Pin & Earrings

ere's a way to showcase coordinating handmade papers—play with colors and designs to create customized jewelry.

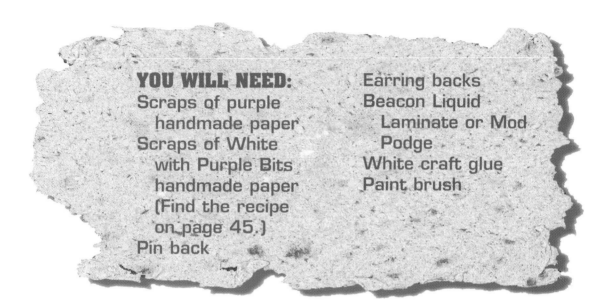

YOU WILL NEED:
Scraps of purple
    handmade paper
Scraps of White
    with Purple Bits
    handmade paper
    (Find the recipe
    on page 45.)
Pin back

Earring backs
Beacon Liquid
    Laminate or Mod
    Podge
White craft glue
Paint brush

1. Using the straight edge of a ruler as a guide, tear one 3" triangle and two 1½" triangles from the purple paper and one 1½" triangle, two 1" triangles, and one ½" triangle from the white paper.

2. To make the pin, glue a 1½" and ½" white triangle on the 3" purple triangle as shown.

3. To make each of the earrings, glue a 1" triangle on a 1½" purple triangle as shown.

4. Paint six coats of liquid laminate on both sides of all pieces, allowing them to dry completely on each side and between coats.

5. Glue the pin back on the back of the large purple triangle and an earring back on each of the smaller purple triangles.

Position the triangles on the pin and earrings.

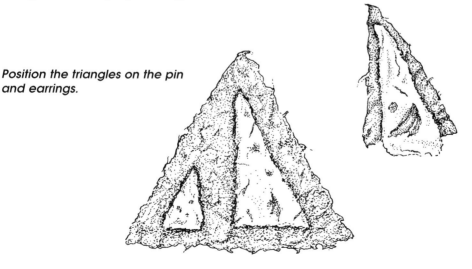

Watercolor Print Note Cards

The watercolor effect on these lovely note cards is accomplished during the couching stage (refer to the directions on page 31). The design is limited only by the paper napkin designs available and your imagination. You can create beautiful handmade cards with a watercolor effect without touching a paint brush!

YOU WILL NEED:
1/8 cup cotton linter pulp or recycled paper pulp (this will make one sheet)
Floral paper napkin
Plain paper in coordinating color
Straight edge ruler
Craft knife
White craft glue

1. Screen one 5" x 7" sheet of paper from the pulp and couch to a dry felt.

2. Cut or tear a floral design from the paper napkin.

3. Center the torn floral design face up along the bottom edge of the wet sheet of handmade paper and cover with a dry felt.

Position the torn floral design on the handmade sheet.

4. Use a rolling pin to press out water and embed the paper napkin into the handmade paper.

5. Place the paper on a flat surface and allow to dry.

6. Measure and cut a plain sheet of paper approximately 1/2" smaller than the handmade sheet.

7. Fold both the handmade paper and the plain paper in half and glue the plain sheet of paper along the inside fold of the handmade paper. (If the handmade paper is smooth enough to write on, you may not need to add the plain paper.)

Glue writing paper inside the folded handmade paper card.

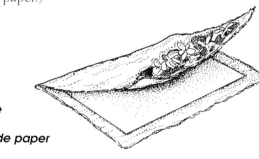

Paper Covered Eggs

$\mathcal{H}$ere's a great way to use all those beautiful scraps of paper from other projects. Cover plastic foam eggs or balls and place them in a bowl or basket as an accent for your decor or for a holiday table. The following instructions are for one egg only.

1. Choose scraps of handmade paper in a pleasing color combination. Arrange the pieces of paper on the egg form, using straight pins to secure.

2. Use Fabri Tac to glue the paper pieces to the egg form, overlapping or tearing paper as needed.

3. Tuck the end of the ribbon under the edge of a piece of paper and glue. Allow to dry.

4. Wrap the ribbon around the egg randomly, occasionally dabbing a spot of glue on as needed to secure it.

Paper pieces secured to the egg form with pins.

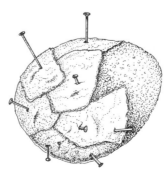

Blanket Stitched Paper Lampshade

*T*his lampshade incorporates eight different sheets of handmade paper. The coordinating lavender and purple sheets on the shade are finished with a blanket stitch and laced together. Two larger white handmade sheets cover the lamp base. Using a lamp kit makes this project extra easy, but you can cover a lamp you already own by measuring the lampshade and making a pattern from those measurements.

The first sheet of handmade paper is made from a base of white pulp with purple pulp scattered on top just before screening to make large purple splotches on it. When you screen the next sheet, the purple pulp will break up and mix with the white, creating a pale lavender sheet with smaller bits of purple. The next sheet will be deeper purple with less distinctive bits and so on. If you add more white or cotton linter pulp, the

sheets may have white spots on purple paper.

These papers show how adding to the pulp can produce different looks with each sheet screened.

YOU WILL NEED:
8 sheets of coordinating handmade papers for the lampshade
2 sheets white handmade paper for the lamp base

Adhesive lamp and lampshade kit (available as a set or separately)
Coordinating pearl cotton thread, size 5
Chenille needle

1. Use the manufacturer's pattern for the lampshade. Divide the pattern into eighths and make a pattern of one of the eighths. Reduce the size by ¼" on each lengthwise side of the pattern.

2. Using the new pattern, cut eight pieces from the coordinating handmade papers. Check the size by laying the pieces on top of the manufacturer's pattern, allowing for ¼" between the pieces for stitching and lacing.

Make a new pattern from the manufacturer's pattern, then use an ⅛ of it to cut out eight pieces of handmade paper.

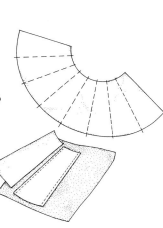

3. Thread a chenille needle with pearl cotton thread and blanket stitch around the edges of each handmade paper piece.

Blanket stitch.

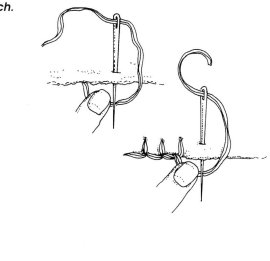

*Fit the pattern
pieces
together.*

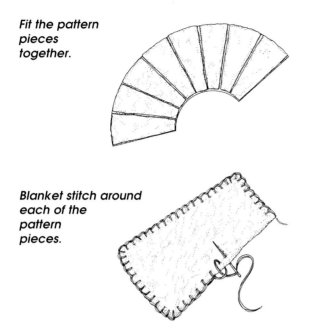

*Leave two edges
unlaced until you
check the fit on
the lampshade.*

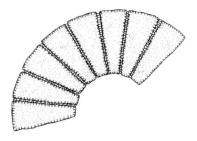

*Blanket stitch around
each of the
pattern
pieces.*

6. When all eight pieces are laced together, check for fit by positioning the laced paper shade on the lampshade. If you need to alter the paper shade for fit, you can make small adjustments in the lacing, which is somewhat elastic.

7. Refer to the manufacturer's instructions and remove the paper covering the adhesive on the shade. Carefully fit the laced paper shade over the adhesive, smoothing and adjusting it as needed.

4. Again, lay the stitched pieces on the manufacturer's pattern to check the size. If the pieces are larger than the pattern, cut them to size. If they're smaller, you'll need to make adjustments when you do the lacing.

5. Determine how you want to position each of the laced pieces on the lampshade and lace them together.

8. Follow the manufacturer's directions to cover the lamp base with white handmade paper. Most lamp kits are designed for fabric coverings, but your lovely handmade paper will work just as well.

*Lace the pattern
pieces together.*

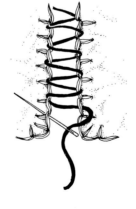

Hand-Cast Projects

Hand-cast projects are easy and fun to make. With a minimum of work, you can produce beautiful delicate paper castings from cookie cutters, gelatin and candy molds, or any of the paper molds now readily available on the market. Paper castings are beautiful in their natural state or decorated with paint, glitter, and ribbons.

Use these lovely paper castings as ornaments, sachet holders, to decorate packages, stationery, papier mâché boxes, or even as unique pieces of jewelry.

Golden Hearts Garland

Assembling this project is quick and easy, but allow plenty of time for drying. The poured hearts must be completely dry before dipping them in the liquid glitter. After dipping, allow at least 24 hours drying time before stringing them.

It's a good idea to pour extra hearts in case one gets damaged during the dipping or stringing process.

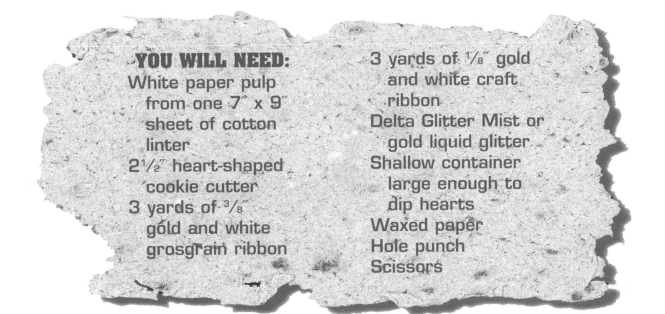

1. Using the heart-shaped cookie cutter as a mold, pour 18 hearts from white paper pulp. Refer to page 29 for pouring directions. Allow the hearts to dry thoroughly.

2. Shake the liquid glitter to blend and pour approximately ½″ liquid into the shallow container.

3. Carefully dip each heart into the liquid glitter, turning it over to cover both sides. Be careful, the paper will become extremely fragile when wet. If too much glitter collects on the paper, gently it dab off with a paper towel. Place the hearts on waxed paper to dry.

4. When the liquid glitter is completely dry (at least 24 hours) use a hole punch to punch two holes, approximately ½″ apart, in the top of each heart.

5. String the hearts onto the grosgrain ribbon, threading the ribbon from back to front and leaving a space of 3″ between hearts.

String the hearts on the ribbon to make a garland.

6. Cut 18 5″ lengths of craft ribbon.

7. Fold each 5″ piece of ribbon in half and thread it around the garland ribbon and through the loop, forming a lark's head knot. Trim the ends of the ribbons.

Tie lark's head knots.

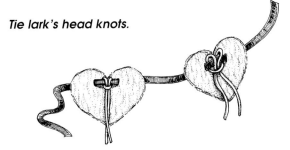

Sunny Dream Catcher

This hand-cast sun was made with a gelatin mold. You can choose from a variety of motifs—whatever is in your kitchen cupboard or craft workshop.

You'll be surprised at the number of molds you already have that can be used for hand-casting. To frame the sun, simply wrap a wooden embroidery hoop in raffia.

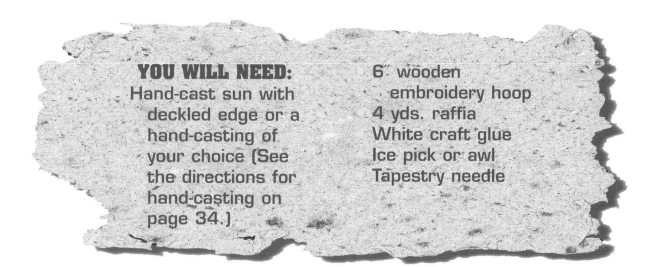

YOU WILL NEED:
Hand-cast sun with
  deckled edge or a
  hand-casting of
  your choice (See
  the directions for
  hand-casting on
  page 34.)

6" wooden
  embroidery hoop
4 yds. raffia
White craft glue
Ice pick or awl
Tapestry needle

1. Loosely wrap raffia around the inner circle of the embroidery hoop, leaving a 6" tail at the beginning and end for tying. To prevent the raffia from unwinding, apply random dabs of white craft glue where necessary.

Wrap the embroidery hoop with raffia.

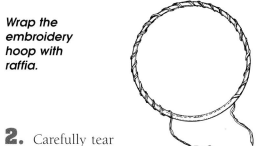

2. Carefully tear around the edge of the hand-cast sun so that the sun is approximately ½" smaller than the diameter of the embroidery hoop.

Place the sun in the hoop.

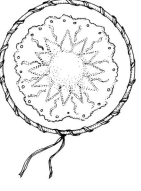

3. Measure and mark approximately 1" intervals around the paper circle and approximately ½" from the edge of the paper.

4. Using an ice pick or awl, punch holes at each mark.

5. Thread a tapestry needle with raffia and thread the raffia through the loop of raffia on the inside of the hoop, then through the first hole in the sun and back to the raffia on the hoop. Begin at the top of the hoop and continue around the sun, loosely lacing the sun inside the hoop.

Lace the sun in place.

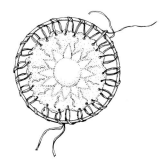

6. Tie the ends of the raffia on the hoop to form a loop for hanging.

Hand-Cast
Stars

Use these hand-cast stars mounted on corrugated cardboard for gift tags or as ornaments. You'll want to make lots of these to decorate your Christmas packages and tree. Look for a mold that has several stars on one mold—a candy mold or a mold specifically designed for papermaking is probably your best bet.

Don't limit yourself to stars—try casting other small designs such as flowers and hearts. You can also use this idea to decorate the front of a guest book or for place cards.

YOU WILL NEED:
Hand-cast stars (See the directions for hand-casting on page 34.)
Gold glitter fabric paint
Gold metallic thread
Corrugated cardboard
Paint brush
Craft knife or scissors
White craft glue
Chenille needle
Scissors

1. Paint each hand-cast star with gold glitter fabric paint. Allow to dry.

2. Cut a 2" x 3" piece of corrugated cardboard.

3. Glue the hand-cast star on the corrugated cardboard.

4. Thread a chenille needle with gold metallic thread and run the needle through one corner of the card. Tie a generous loop and trim.

5. To use as a gift tag or place card, write on the back of the cardboard.

Gold Star Brooch

A tiny hand-cast star is a simple and elegant fashion accent. This star, accented with gold glitter paint, makes a lovely and inexpensive brooch.

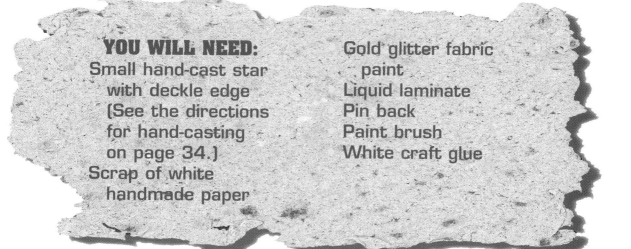

YOU WILL NEED:
Small hand-cast star
    with deckle edge
    (See the directions
    for hand-casting
    on page 34.)
Scrap of white
    handmade paper
Gold glitter fabric
    paint
Liquid laminate
Pin back
Paint brush
White craft glue

1. Paint gold glitter fabric paint on the hand-cast star and allow to dry.

2. Tear a piece of white handmade paper to match the outside deckled edge of the hand-cast star and glue it to the back of the hand-cast star.

3. Paint three coats of liquid laminate on all sides of the star and paper, allowing each coat to dry completely before painting the next.

4. Glue the pin back to the back of the hand-cast star.

The hand-cast star above the paper backing.

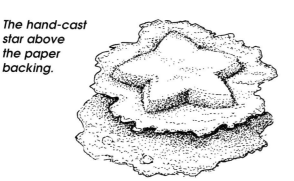

Dove Box

Cover a papier mâché box with a white lace paper doily, add a lattice braid and a hand-cast paper dove and viola! You've created an elegant trinket box.

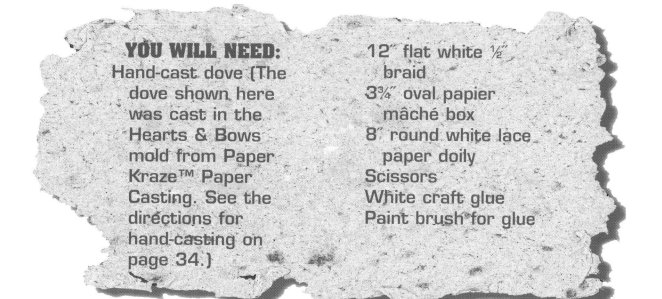

YOU WILL NEED:
Hand-cast dove (The dove shown here was cast in the Hearts & Bows mold from Paper Kraze™ Paper Casting. See the directions for hand-casting on page 34.)

12" flat white ½" braid
3¾" oval papier mâché box
8" round white lace paper doily
Scissors
White craft glue
Paint brush for glue

1. Measure the diameter and height of the papier mâché box. Cut a strip from the doily that is ½" longer than the diameter and ½" shorter than the box height. The box lid won't fit properly if the doily extends to the top edge of the box.

2. Paint thinned white craft glue on the doily strip and glue it around the box bottom, aligning the bottom edges. Overlap the ends of the strip where they meet. Allow to dry.

Glue the doily around the papier mâché box.

3. Use the box lid to draw a pattern and cut it out of the doily to cover the lid.

4. Paint thinned white craft glue on the doily and glue it to the top of the box lid. Allow to dry.

5. Glue the braid on the lid's rim, centering it all around the rim. Overlap the ends slightly, trim, and glue in place.

Glue the braid around the box lid.

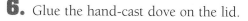

6. Glue the hand-cast dove on the lid.

Rose Petal Potpourri Heart

Rose petals and bits of a golden doily make a lovely potpourri framed by a hand-cast heart. This gilded hand-cast paper heart is finished with a golden cord for hanging.

YOU WILL NEED:

Hand-cast paper heart with deckled edge (The heart shown was cast in the Heart Frame mold by Cotton Press™ Terra Cotta Molds. See directions for hand-casting on page 34.)

Gold metallic acrylic paint

5" square of tulle

1 tablespoon of dried rose petals

8" round white paper lace doily

Gold paper doily

12" length of ¼" gold cord

Hole punch

Paint brush

Stencil

White craft glue

Pinking shears

Scissors

1. Use scissors to carefully cut out the inside of the hand-cast heart to make a frame. If you used the Cotton Press mold, cut in the groove between the decorative outside of the frame and the inside beading.

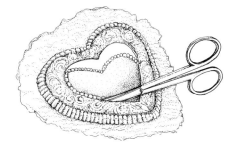

Trim the inside of the hand-cast heart with scissors.

2. Use a dry stencil brush to lightly brush gold metallic acrylic paint on the raised design of the hand-cast paper heart frame. Allow to dry.

HOT TIP

Use small sewing or manicure scissors to cut the heart from the center of the hand-cast heart.

3. Center the piece of tulle on the back side of the heart and glue it along the inside edges. Allow to dry.

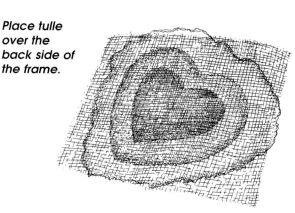

Place tulle over the back side of the frame.

4. Carefully trim away the excess tulle so it won't show along the outside edge.

5. Make gold circles by using a hole punch to punch holes from the gold doily. Mix the gold holes with dried rose petals to create the potpourri.

6. Lay the heart on a flat surface, front side down, and put the potpourri in the center of the tulle.

7. To make the backing for the heart, cover the potpourri with the white doily and glue the doily to the heart frame. Apply the glue to the entire surface of the frame, not just the edges. Allow to dry.

8. Trim the doily and the deckle edge of the handmade paper heart with pinking shears.

Trim away the deckled edge of the heart with pinking shears.

Trim the tulle and place rose petal potpourri in the center.

9. Punch a hole in the center top of the heart and thread the gold cord through the hole and knot.

Paper pulp clings to almost anything—including wire—which makes for these unusual and delicate sculptures and wire ornaments. You may want to begin your wire and paper experiments using purchased wire baskets from craft or garden supply stores—there are so many new and unusual shapes available.

Use these wire and paper projects as the basis for making your own original creations. Both the basket and pedestal are chicken wire, rolled and twisted into shape. The wreaths, hearts, and angels are fashioned from coiled wire, dipped in paper pulp and then embellished with paint, ribbons, and dried flowers. Use your imagination to create one-of-a-kind wire sculptures. Keep your eyes open for "dippable" items—the simplest twig can be transformed into a unique sculpture.

Before beginning, read through the dipping instructions on page 37.

Wire & Paper Basket

Paper doesn't have to be in sheets or hand-cast. Here the paper pulp is used with wire to make an unusual basket. Try different shapes of wire structures and vary the pulp to create your own unique basket.

You will need:
Vat of white cotton
   linter paper pulp
   (90% water to
   10% pulp)
12" x 48" piece of
   floral netting or
   small-gauge
   chicken wire
Wire thread
Acrylic sealer
   and/or acrylic
   paint (optional)
Work gloves
Wire cutters

1. If you are using coated floral netting, remove as much of the green coating as possible by bending, shaking, and scraping it off.

2. Wearing gloves, use the wire cutters to cut a 12" x 36" section of wire and form it into a cylinder, butting the ends together.

Form the wire into a cylinder.

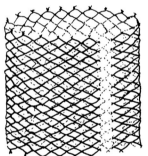

3. Use the wire thread to whip-stitch the butted ends together. Bend under any sharp edges and trim the wire ends with wire cutters.

Loop a tin wire over and through ends to secure.

4. To form the bottom of the basket, bend the wire to the center of the cylinder at approximately the halfway point. When you are satisfied with the bottom, use wire thread to join the edges. Bend any sharp ends under to finish off the bottom.

Bend the wire into the center to form the bottom of the basket.

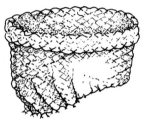

5. To form the sides, roll the top edges under and down to the inside of the cylinder. Continue rolling and bending down until the sides are the desired height and shape.

Roll and bend the wire to the inside of the basket to form the sides.

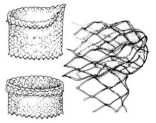

6. Begin dipping by submersing the wire into a vat of paper pulp. Allow the basket to dry completely and dip again. Continue this dipping and drying process until you're happy with the coverage.

7. You can seal the basket by painting on acrylic sealer or paint. Although this won't waterproof the basket, it does help protect it against dampness and gives it strength.

Dipped Pedestal

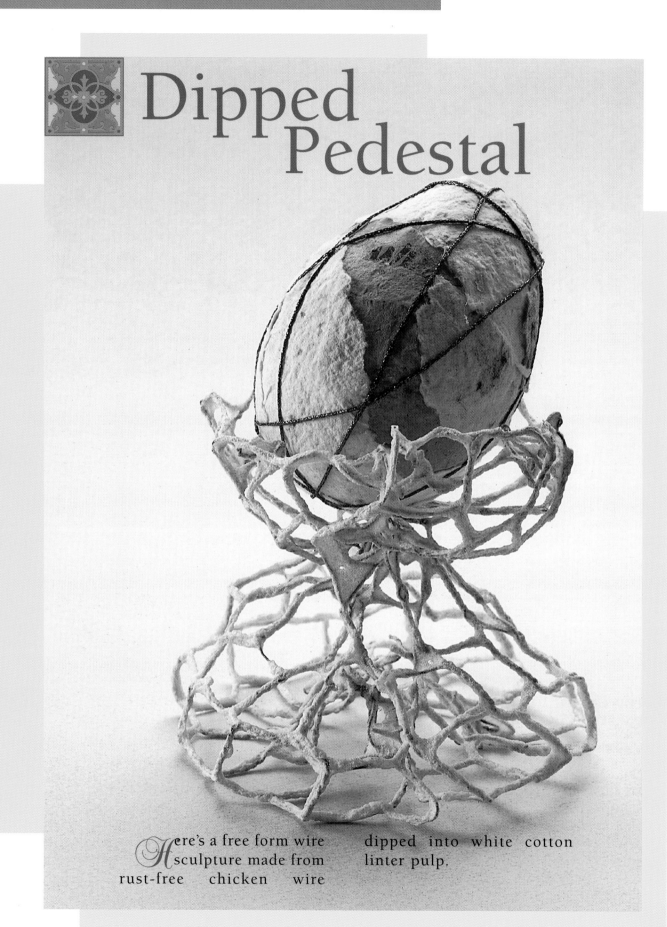

Here's a free form wire sculpture made from rust-free chicken wire dipped into white cotton linter pulp.

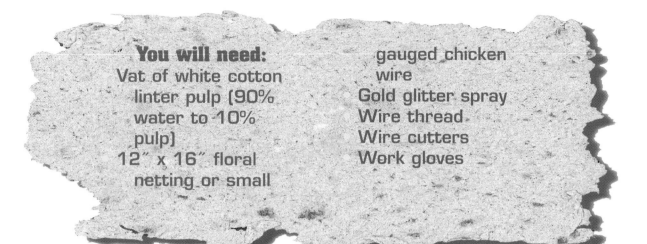

You will need:
Vat of white cotton
linter pulp (90%
water to 10%
pulp)
12″ x 16″ floral
netting or small

gauged chicken
wire
Gold glitter spray
Wire thread
Wire cutters
Work gloves

1. If you are using coated floral netting, remove as much of the green coating as possible by bending, shaking, and scraping it off.

2. Form the wire into a cylinder, butting the ends together.

Form the wire into a cylinder.

3. Whip-stitch the butted ends together with wire thread. Bend under any sharp ends and trim the ends with a wire cutter.

Loop a thin wire over and through the ends to secure them.

4. Form the bottom of the pedestal by bending the wire to the center of the cylinder at approximately 4″ from the bottom of the cylinder. The bottom center will be pushed up into the cylinder center.

5. Finish the top edge by folding it approximately 1″ toward the center of the cylinder and rolling the wire edge under.

Roll and bend the wire to the inside of the pedestal to form the sides.

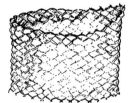

6. Squeeze the wire to the center of the cylinder to form an hour glass shape.

Make an hour glass shape by squeezing the cylinder together in the center.

7. Dip the wire armature into the vat of pulp. Refer to the dipping instructions on page 38. Let each coat of pulp dry before redipping. Continue to dip the armature until you are pleased with the coverage.

8. Spray the dried sculpture with gold glitter.

Wire and Paper Ornaments

ine wire can be shaped into wreaths, hearts and angels to dip into pulp. This creates unusual and delicate ornaments. Begin with the wreaths and then shape your wire into heart and angel shapes. These ornaments look lovely on a tree or as part of the gift wrapping on a special package.

Wreath & Heart Shaped Ornament

You will need:
Vat of white cotton linter pulp
24 gauge galvanized rust-free wire (1 yard per ornament)
1" dowels
¾" dowels
Wire cutters
Needle nose pliers
Work gloves

1. Begin approximately 2" from one end of a 36" piece of wire and wrap the wire around a ¾" dowel to form a circle. Using needle nose pliers, twist the wire to hold the circle shape.

Wrap wire around a dowel.

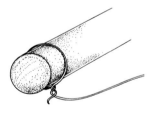

2. Place the circle at the left end of the dowel, just above the dowel with a length of wire pointing down. Coil the wire around the dowel.

Coil the wire around the dowel.

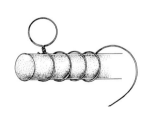

3. Remove the coiled wire from the dowel and stretch the coil to a 9" length.

4. Press the coils flat with your fingers and form the flattened coil into a circle.

Flatten the coil into a circle.

5. Join the wire ends by twisting the end of the coiled wire around the wire just below the original circle.

6. To shape the circle, wrap the flattened coil around a 2" round shape. To shape the heart, push the center top down until it looks like a heart.

7. Trim the sharp ends.

8. Dip the wire ornament into paper pulp and allow to dry. If you want a thicker coating of pulp, dip it again and let it dry completely.

9. Embellish with ribbon, thread, glitter, fabric paint, spray glitter mist, dried flowers, or whatever you desire.

Angel Shaped Ornament

1. Find the center of a 36" piece of wire and form a circle around a ¾" dowel. Twist and shape the wire to form a circle for the angel's halo.

2. In line and directly below the halo, form a 1" circle for the angel's head.

3. Bend each wire end away from the center.

Shape the wire into two circles—one for the halo and one for the head.

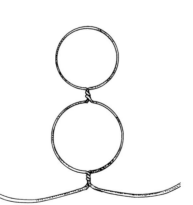

4. Beginning as close to the angel's head as possible, twist one of the wire ends around a ¾" dowel to form a coil. Repeat with the other wire end on the other side.

5. Remove the coiled wire from the dowel and stretch the coil to a 9" length.

6. Press the coils flat with your fingers and form the flattened coil into a circle.

7. Shape the circles into wings.

8. Join the ends of the wire by twisting the end of the coiled wires around the twisted wire just below the head.

9. Shape the halo into a heart by pushing down at the center top of the circle.

10. Dip the wire angel into paper pulp and allow to dry. If you want a thicker coating of pulp, dip it again and let it dry completely.

11. Embellish with ribbon, thread, glitter, fabric paint, spray glitter mist, dried flowers, or whatever you desire.

About The Author

Nancy Worrell discovered crafts at the age of two, threading button necklaces while her grandmother sewed. Through both grandmothers and her mother, Nancy was also introduced to embroidery, crocheting, quilting, and painting. These skills were used to clothe three daughters, decorate a home, and provide unique gifts for friends and relatives.

Nancy continues to explore crafts, learning and combining new techniques and skills with those already acquired. Several years ago, a neighbor introduced her to papermaking and Nancy discovered yet another way to express her creativity and use her crafting skills.

Nancy relates to the paper as if it is fabric—molding, stitching, and combining it with fabrics, ribbons, and lace. Paper also allows Nancy to incorporate her love of gardening, using dried flowers and leaves in many handmade paper projects.

For the past seven years, Nancy has been sharing her creative projects through publication in national craft magazines and books.

Photo by Paul Bass

Glossary

Bast fiber: Fibers derived from the inner bark of plants. Flax, hemp, jute, ramie, okra, and kudzu are examples.

Bleed: Ink running into the lines of the fibers of the paper causing a feathery look to ink-drawn lines. Also, the discoloration caused by the pigment of rose petals or other natural materials.

Canvas stretcher bars: Wood strips cut to fit together to form a frame for stretching canvas. Available at most art supply stores.

Cellulose: Substance found in the cell wall of most plants and important in the manufacture of paper.

Chenille needle: Sharp-pointed, long-eyed needle used for stitching heavy threads.

Colander: Kitchen utensil with holes for draining off liquids.

Cotton linter: Coarse short fibers of cotton, too short for thread-spinning, which are used for making paper pulp.

Couching: Transferring a sheet of newly made wet paper pulp from the mold to a felt or other surface.

Craft knife: Utility knife used for cutting cardboard and foam board. A common brand name is X-acto Knife.

Deckle: Wooden frame that is placed on top of the mold to contain the pulp during screening. The size of the sheet of paper will be determined by the interior dimension of the deckle.

Deckle edge: Rough edge created by the deckle or the edge around the outside of a hand-cast mold. This edge is characteristic of handmade paper.

Felt: Absorbent fabric piece onto which a newly formed sheet is couched.

Flax: Plant native to Eurasia. Major source of cloth fiber before cotton. The fiber from the stems are used to make linen and paper.

Foam board: Lightweight rigid board used for making design templates.

Gelatin: Substance used in sizing. See sizing.

Hand-casting: Process of pressing pulp into a mold and letting it dry before demolding.

Kaolin: White clay in powder form used in hand-cast paper to produce a stronger cast with a smooth, glossy surface.

Laminating: Bonding together two or more sheets for extra thickness or decorative effect.

Miter: Diagonal joint where two pieces of paper meet at a corner.

Mold: 1. Screen covered frame that forms the sheet of paper. The deckle is used on top of the mold and contains the pulp on the mold during screening. 2. Form for hand-casting pulp into a shape, such as a gelatin mold or muffin tin.

Papyrus: Aquatic reed used by the Egyptians and Greeks to make a form of paper. The word paper is derived from the word papyrus.

Parchment: Skin of a sheep or goat prepared for writing or painting.

Pearl cotton thread: Twisted non-divisible cotton thread used for embroidery and needlepoint.

Pulp: Substance of beaten (or blended) fiber and water used to make paper.

Pulping: Process of beating or blending fiber and water to pulp.

Screening: Process of dipping the deckle and mold into the pulp and collecting the pulp on the mold screen. Another phrase often used for this process is "pulling a sheet of paper."

Sizing: Substance added to paper to reduce absorbency, thereby reducing or preventing inks from bleeding. May be added to pulp during papermaking or applied to finished sheet. Common sizing agents include gelatin, starch, and cellulose.

Tapestry needle: Needle with blunt rounded point and long oval eye to use for large or several strands of thread.

Tulle: Extra fine nylon net often used for wedding veils.

Vat: Rustproof, watertight container used to hold pulp and for floating a deckle and mold for the pouring method.

Suppliers

*I*f you are unable to find any of these products in your local craft or art supply store, here are some mail order sources for most of the supplies needed to complete the projects in this book.

Barron Enterprises
(800) 756-9473
http://www.cottonpress.com/crafts/

Manufacturer and supplier of terra cotta molds including the Heart Frame mold used in the Rose Petal Potpourri Heart on page 104. Visit their web site for additional information about hand-cast paper, to see their molds, and for ordering.

Colorado Blossoms
1501 Rancho Way
Loveland, CO 80537
(970) 669-4578

Naturally grown and pressed flowers, herbs, and foliage available in packages and sheets.

Craft Catalog
P.O. Box 1069
Reynoldsburg, OH 43068
(800) 777-1442

Craft Catalog carries papermaking supplies, fabric paints, wooden trays, jewelry findings, and papier mâché boxes.

Greg Markim, Inc.
P.O. Box 13245
Milwaukee, WI 53213
(800) 453-1485

Manufacturer of the Arnold Grummer's Papermill, a complete papermaking kit. The deckle and mold in this kit is specifically designed for pouring. Also available is a kit with an envelope template and a tin can papermaking kit

Munro Corp.
3954 West Twelve Mile Road
Berkley, MI 48072
(800) 638-0543

Distributor for Kiti Craft Adhesive Decorator Lamps.

Paper Chase
P.O. Box 16555
Kansas City, MO 64133
(813) 356-4606

Papermaking kits and clay molds for hand-casting.

Bibliography

Books

Hunter, Dard, *Papermaking: The History and Technique of an Ancient Craft.* New York: Dover Publications, Inc., 1947. An indepth history of papermaking.

Toale, Bernard, *The Art of Papermaking.* Worcester, Massachusetts: Davis Publications, Inc., 1983.

Blake, Kathy & Milne, Bill, *Making & Decorating Your Own Paper.* Sterling Publishing Co., Inc., 1994.

Shannon, Faith, *The Art and Craft of Paper.* Chronicle Books, 1994.

Hauser, Priscilla, *Create Your Own Greeting Cards & Gift Wrap with Priscilla Hauser.* North Light Books, 1994.

Dawson, Sophie, *The Art and Craft of Papermaking.* Running Press, 1992.

Lillian Bell, *Plant Fibers for Papermaking.* Lilliaceae Press, 1981. A reference for those interested in using plant fibers.

Other Resources

The Robert C. William's American Museum of Papermaking. The museum is located at the Institute of Paper and Science Technology, 500 10th Street NW, Atlanta, GA 30318-5794. Hours of operation 8:30 a.m. to 5:00 p.m. Monday through Friday. Or take a tour through their virtual museum at http://www.IPST.edu/AMP/.

Investigate local art guilds, and craft schools for workshops and programs offered in papermaking. Also check out the continuing education classes offered at junior colleges and universities for classes in papermaking.

Index

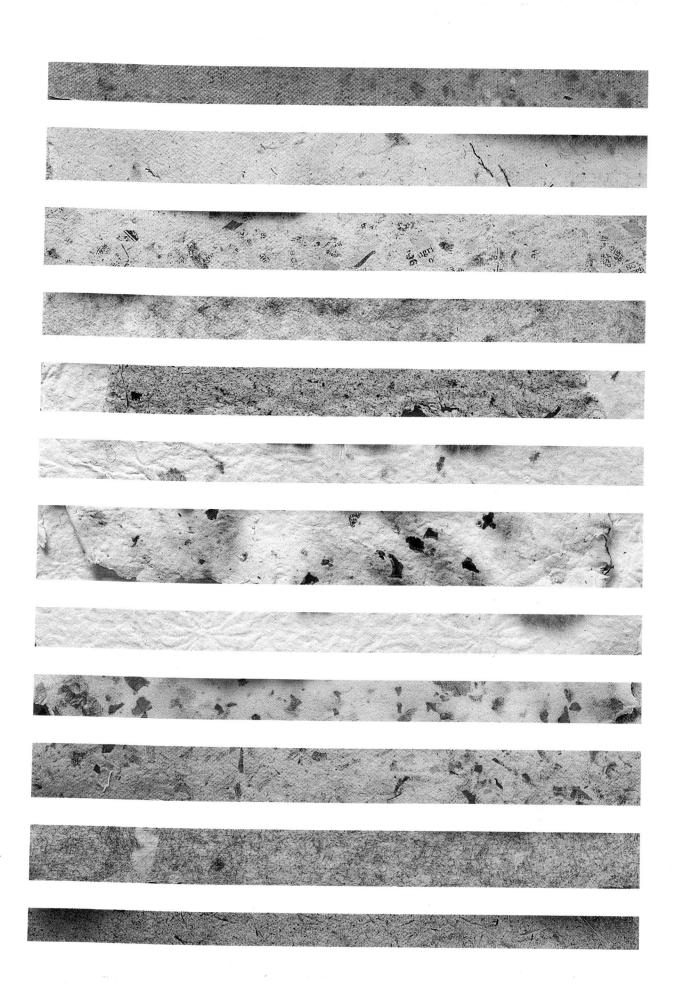

INDULGE YOUR CREATIVITY
LET US SHOW YOU HOW!

Krause Publications
*Bringing your
hobby home!*

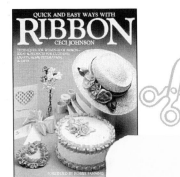

Quick and Easy Ways w...
by Ceci Johnson
Just 30 minutes is all you'll...
one of the 24 projects outlin...
Perfect flat borders, pleats,...
flowers and weaving. Tie th...
together for pretty ornamen...
accessories and colorful gi...
8-1/4x10-7/8 SC • 96p • 8p...
• **QEWWR $14.95**

...porary Decoupage
...eas for Gifts, Keepsakes, and
...urnishings
...Barker
...searching for a fresh approach to
...craft, check out this collection of
...n 35 innovative decoupage pro-
...he home. Color photographs fur-
...ain detailed instructions that com-
...ert advice on techniques, equip-
*...ONUS! Six sheets of ready-to-pho-
...ecoupage motifs included.*
...-7/8 SC • 112p • color throughout
...$19.95

The Crafter's Guide...
by Tammy Young
Finally, a book that sorts...
ing array of glues, adhes...
webs. Choose the right...
and learn how to bond...
faces of any sort. Chapt...
practice solving the stick...
8-1/4x10-7/8 SC • 96p •...
• **CGTG $14.95**

...Craft
...of Creative Ideas for
...ng on Cards, Clothing,
...re, and More
...Haysom
...ace is up for grabs with stamping.
...nd small scale objects alike take on
...nensions when customized stamp-
...s over. See just how easy and ver-
...amping is with these 40 examples
...for beginners and stampaholics
...1/4x10-7/8 SC • 128p • color
...out • **STCR $19.95**

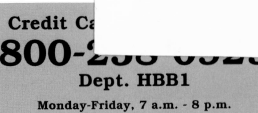

...AUTIFUL CRAFTS
...BE A SECRET!
...GIFT OF BOOKS
TO A FRIEND!

SATISFACTION GUARANTEE
If for any reason you are not completely satisfied
with your purchase, simply return it within 14 days
and receive a full refund, less shipping.